COMING HOME

~

20 GLIMPSES FROM THE ROAD OF RETURN IN MODERN AMERICA

COMING
HOME

ISRAEL BOOKSHOP
LAKEWOOD, NJ

20 GLIMPSES FROM THE ROAD OF RETURN IN MODERN AMERICA

Compiled by the Bostoner Rebbe,
Rabbi Levi Yitzchak Horowitz shlit'a

Copyright © 2005

ISBN 1-931681-64-3

Cover design by: Ben Gasner
Book design by: Sruly Perl @ Connections 845.371.2222
Edited by: Yisroel Asher
Proofread by: Nachum Lemberg

Dist. by: ISRAEL BOOK SHOP
501 Prospect St.
Lakewood, N.J. 08701

Tel. 732.901.3009 • 888.536.7427
Fax 732.901.4012
email: isrbkshp@aol.com

Printed by:
Gross Bros. Printing

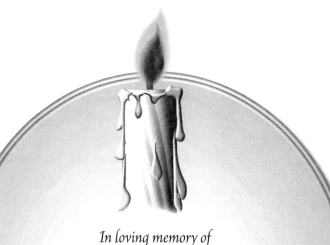

In loving memory of

The Bostoner Rebbetzin

Raichel Horowitz, a"h

Whose passing on 16 Taamuz 5762 (16 June 2002) was mourned by the many hundreds of families, from all walks of life, whose lives were transformed by her warm smile, parental concern, sage advice and enduring kindness.

A woman of inconceivable strength, selflessness and self-sacrifice, she unhesitatingly dedicated her entire life to helping others.

Combining rare nobility, unfeigned friendliness and super-human effort, she modestly gave new meaning to the lives of future generations of Jews, both within and outside of the Bostoner Chassidic community.

The descendant of great Rebbeim and the devoted wife and dedicated partner of the Bostoner Rebbe,

R. Levi Yitzchock Horowitz, shlita,

she left her many children, grandchildren, great-grandchildren, Chassidim and friends an inspiring legacy of service and love. May her memory be a blessing.

לזכרון עולם בהיכל ה׳

This book is dedicated in honor
of our distinguished friends for
many generations

Professor William
and

Bernie Schwartz

by the
New England Chassidic Center

In Memory of

Ann Bakalar

Renowned Philanthropist
of many noble causes.

ת.נ.צ.ב.ה.

TABLE OF CONTENTS

PART 3
YOU'VE GOT IT MADE: PEERS, PRESIDENTS AND PROFESSIONALS

PART 4
THE ROAD BACK TO SINAI

PREFACE
BY THE BOSTONER REBBE

We live in amazing times. We have lived through the destruction of the beautiful Torah edifice that was European Jewry and its rebirth in *Eretz Yisroel*. We have also lived through tragic times of mass assimilation in America and its rebirth in rebuilt day-schools and yeshivas, kollels and communities. Of all this astonishing rebirth, perhaps the most astonishing is the baal teshuvah movement, the return of large numbers of highly committed Jewish men and women to the traditions of their forefathers. I have been privileged to have been able to meet and help many of them, over more than fifty years, and I am still impressed at their determination and ability to return—often from "ground zero," virtually *yesh m'ayin*—to play serious, even prominent roles in the future growth of our people.

Where does such a *zechus* come from? We cannot trace the details, but surely the prayers and tears of long-forgotten generations of pious *zaydes* and *babbehs* were not in vain. And indeed teshuvah links all the generations and man with G-d.

I have encouraged the baalei teshuvah who relate their stories here to make their struggles—often against incredible odds—their *hashgachah pratis* and successes better known. I hope that their sincerity, determination and experiences will inspire you as they have inspired me. For we are all baalei teshuvah or should be. We all need to turn from our limited Divine service of yesterday, determined to reach new levels of spirituality and Divine service tomorrow.

R. LEVI Y. HOROWITZ, *SHLITA*

INTRODUCTION

What do successful young executives, geophysicists and British peerage have in common? What about doctors, photographers and politicians? All are part of a baalei teshuvah phenomenon that is a prominent part of the rebirth and dramatic growth of the American Torah-true religious community. It is a movement of individuals and, thus, one that can only be fully appreciated on the individual level. The twenty, highly personal experiences presented here represent an inspiring glimpse into this highly variegated world of inner heroism and silent victory.

Far from being failures, most were highly successful or getting there—living the American dream—when they found that they needed more. Although talented and committed, their journeys Heavenward were often anything but smooth, a long winding path rather than a six-lane highway. Still, they met the twists and turns with persistence and fortitude—often with help from unexpected quarters—and most of all with the comforting, if sometimes inexplicable, conviction that they were finally... coming home.

The personal nature of teshuvah and the wide variety of experiences reported here make these stories difficult to characterize; although the four sections of this book group them loosely in terms of distance from "home": those whose parents or grandparents still had the *taam* (taste, if not always substance) of observance, those who were "clueless," those who were actively directed away from observance, and those who started life as non-Jews. Since the latter, say our Sages, also stood (spiritually) at Sinai, theirs too is a journey home.

The stories in this collection were written by the protagonists themselves. They are real stories by real people, and to the extent possible, in their own words (although some shortening and editing was unavoidable). As such, they differ somewhat from more tidy renditions in which everything runs smoothly and all swiftly live happily ever after. However, whatever these narratives may lose in childlike simplicity, they gain in adult sincerity, authenticity and impact, for "words from the heart go to the heart."

These stories are more than a look at the admirable and strenuous spiritual efforts of others. They are a challenge to us all. Chassidim still tell of the following conversation between two well-known Chassidic masters. "I always find these summer months difficult," said the first, "for now we read of the sins of *Am Yisroel*" (referring to the golden calf, the spies and the rebellion of *Korach*).

"You're worried about our sins?" said the second, incredulously. "For that we have teshuvah. But what can we do about our *mitzvos*?" What if those lacked sufficient seriousness, intent and effort?

There is still much work to do, and the dedication and sincerity of the baalei teshuvah portrayed can help point the way for us all.

MY GRANDFATHER WOULD
HAVE BEEN PROUD

Behold I will send you Eliyahu HaNavi before the Day of Hashem comes, great and awesome; And He will return the hearts of the fathers to the sons, And the hearts of the sons to their father...
Malachi 3:23-24

The Jewish history of twentieth century America is indeed that of a "melting pot"—in which Reb Itzikel from Europe melted into Mr. Ike and finally Dr. Jason. Within three generations, the complex beauty of centuries of Jewish life and tradition had often melted in the hot sun of materialism and assimilation until little was left. But looks can be deceiving. Under the surface forces were at work—*hashgachah pratis, zechus avos, chasdei Hashem*—slowly, doggedly, seeds sown generations before began to grow again, in ways unknown even to themselves, and, at last, new flowers reached for the sun.

MY FATHER'S TEFILLIN

I n 1926, if I understand correctly, my grandfather made the mistake of his life. He moved with his wife and children and five sons from a rented flat in old, crowded Williamsburg to a new house he had bought in more prosperous Flatbush. The house had a garden next to it, which my grandmother eventually filled with over two hundred rosebushes. The upstairs apartment could be rented out to help pay the mortgage. There was not, at the time, a *balabatish minyan* of the sort he enjoyed; but there was a mammoth Conservative congregation, only two blocks away, that dominated the religious life of the area.

My grandfather was not of the compromising kind. He had come to America as a twenty-year-old tailor, at a time when work that did not involve Shabbos desecration was hard to find. He and his brother-in-law borrowed money and bought a loft and four sewing machines. One half of the loft became a shul; the other became "Sabel and Schaps, Inc., Makers of Men's Coats." They worked longer hours, but they set the schedule. Sabel and Schaps did not work on Shabbos.

Grandfather did not mean to compromise in Flatbush either. In his unfinished basement, he partitioned off a separate room as his private *beis medrash* (study house). He moved all of his books into it: many Yiddish ones, whose details are unknown to me, and a Vilna Shas. He had a study partner on Wednesday nights when, as the boss, he allowed himself to come home early. When the *chazzan* at the Conservative synagogue started saying *na'aritzcha v'nakdishcha* for the *mussaf kedushah*, my grandfather and his sons, taking up a whole row of seats, would stand up and say together the Chassidic (Nusach Ari) version with which he had grown up, *kesser yitnu l'cho*. But Flatbush was not Williamsburg, and his sons could not help being affected by their neighborhood, their friends and their school.

I don't know whether it would have turned out any different in Williamsburg. Many religious couples, in those days, saw their children grow up to be more "American" and less Jewish, and few were able to prevent what seemed to be an inevitable process of assimilation. My father's after-school *cheder* education, as he remembered it, consisted of learning the *alef-beis*, learning to say the *Shmoneh Esrei* without understanding it, and then learning to say it faster. Would Boys' High have left my father any more religious than Madison High did? I will never know.

What I do know is that, after many times standing outside when his friends walked into non-kosher restaurants, one day he finally followed them in. Years afterward, he would refer to that as "the day that G-d failed me." He thought that he should have been struck down by lightning. Apparently his *cheder* rebbe had not warned him that, when a person decides to defile himself, the door is opened for him.

My mother's family was another story; they had been irreligious for so long that they were not even hostile. Before proposing, my father asked mother if she would keep a kosher home and, although the idea was foreign to her, she said yes. She was never comfortable with religion. How could she have been, with no exposure to it but stilted translations, long services she couldn't understand, and her mother-in-law's (largely correct) suspicions that her religious standards were not up to par? But she kept her part of the bargain faithfully, keeping the house kosher and sending us to a Conservative Hebrew School that tried to make us feel good about whatever we might keep, while maintaining a discreet silence about our shortcomings. One by one, my father's brothers also married women less religious than they and, as the Gemara predicts, the influence of the woman on the household was decisive. At least my mother, whatever her own level of observance, never wavered in her willingness to keep a kosher home and to raise her children "Jewish."

My father's *Yiddishkeit* did not wash off easily or entirely, but circumstances eventually took their toll. The U.S. Navy and his stint as a medic in the Second World War finished off his *tefillin*. He worked alternating four-hour shifts, around the clock, on a troop transport with hundreds of sailors of whom only nine were Jews. At first he kept his *tefillin* under his pillow and put them on scrupulously every morning but, in the end, the short rest periods and the needling of the non-Jewish sailors defeated him. When he went off duty, he lay down to rest and the *tefillin* remained where they were. At home they went into a dresser drawer and, as a child, I never knew he had them.

He was still more religious than the people around him. He said *Kiddush* every Friday night, whatever he might do afterward. He went to synagogue on Shabbos, and was always happy when he did. A voracious reader, he was constantly reading books on Jewish topics, and urging them on his more assimilated friends. When I was six months old, he moved the family into the second story of his parents' house.

I was a clever and argumentative child, to my grandfather's great delight. He enjoyed teasing me in order to elicit an argument. "This boy will be a rav," he would say with satisfaction, although nothing in my Conservative education led me to remotely consider the rabbinate. One day I remember seeing him with his *tefillin* on, the first time I had ever seen such a thing. I ran up, in a fright, to my mother to tell her that Grandpa had a black box on his head. She explained to me that he put them on to pray, but that didn't make them seem any less peculiar and frightening. In the Talmud, Rabbi Eliezer says that the verse, "And all the nations of the earth (*amei ha-aretz*) shall see that the name of Hashem is called upon you, and they shall be afraid of you," refers to wearing *tefillin* on one's head. In this case, the frightened *amei ha-aretz*—which can also mean "ignoramus"—surely included me!

I knew that we weren't keeping everything that Jews should keep. I knew some things we were not supposed to do on Shabbos, though not much about what we *were* supposed to do. It bothered me to pray, "May those who keep Shabbos rejoice in Your Kingship," when I knew that I wasn't on the receiving end of those blessings. Occasionally, I would joke nervously with my father about keeping kosher only at home. "Not only will we go to Hell," I said—truly assimilated in my choice of terms—"but we won't even have a place to live in Hell, because our kosher house will be in Heaven!" One day my father surprised me by admitting that he didn't like eating that *treif* stuff, either. "Let's make a deal," he said, "that neither of us will eat it."

Grandpa passed away when I was ten, a loss that I took with the swiftly passing sadness that is as close as children come to mourning a relative whose death does not change their daily routine. Of Grandpa's six sons, not one could read the books that filled his basement *beis medrash*. They gave them to Cousin Gershon, an Orthodox rabbi and a professor, the nearest scholarly relative they had. At the *seder*, where Grandpa had always sat up front with his sons and grandchildren around him, my father now presided, the eldest of his brothers.

Father introduced a few innovations: instead of reading everything together in a speedy chant, he had each member of the family read a bit aloud in English, the only language they all understood. I was a little scandalized, little suspecting that the *Tosafot* make a similar suggestion. However, I really liked his other innovation, having me sit at his right hand and sing in a loud voice any part that I happened to have learned in Hebrew school. I was always a sucker for *kavod*, and I loved my father's *seder*. I could not understand how my cousins, as they grew into teenagers, could stop wanting to come every year.

At Hebrew school educational standards were not particularly high, but I met them with relish. By my Bar Mitzvah I already knew the first blessing of the Grace after Meals by heart, which put me far ahead of my contemporaries. The *shamash* of the shul taught us how to put on *tefillin*, but he didn't tell us exactly what one was supposed to do once they were on. I was completely unaware of the daily *minyan* that was disguised under the name of the "Kaddish Club." I would have liked to put my *tefillin* on regularly, but I was embarrassed to do so in front of my family. For a few months I would lock my bedroom door, pretending to take a long time getting dressed. There was no way I could read through the hundred pages of the morning prayers, so I decided to take them bit-by-bit. *Mah Tovu* the first day, *Adon Olam* the next, and so on doggedly through the whole service. It lasted until I was through *Shmoneh Esrei* and up to *Tachanun*. Here was a long section that was to be said only on Mondays and Thursdays. Well, it *was* a Monday, so I started it, but I couldn't finish it. The next day was a Tuesday, of course. Should I finish it? Skip to the next part? In confusion I put my *tefillin* away, and soon got out of the habit entirely.

I was still thirteen when my mother's father fell ill, an infection as unexpected as it was severe. I prayed to Hashem to save him, but nagging questions undermined my attention. What should Hashem save him *for*? He was not religious, so he would not be fulfilling more *mitzvos*. He was about to retire, so he would not be useful to people at his job. He was human, and so he would die in any case. In the day or two of those prayers, I came to appreciate that we can never truly save a life, only prolong it, and that, in the long run, the most important question is not how long we live but what we do with the time we have. I thought I knew what was important in life—after all, I was *thirteen* already—but my previous ambition to be a doctor began to fade.

When I went away to college, my father sent with me a Hertz *Chumash* and an English translation of the *Kitzur Shulchan Aruch*, hardly a well-stocked Jewish library but significantly more than the other Jews there had. Religion was not even frowned upon; it was simply not under consideration at all. A friend once asked me if I believed in G-d. "Well, I don't know," I said carefully. "I can see that there are problems with the idea, but I think that He *might* exist." "Wow," said my scandalized friend. "I mean, except for that, you're so *normal!*"

I did not find Conservative Judaism intellectually satisfying. If Hashem did *not* give the Torah, why do we go to all the trouble of keeping part of it? And if He *did*, what possible good could come of violating all the other parts? Nevertheless, in the natural course of events, I would probably have remained a Conservative Jew to the end, silencing any moral demands with the all-purpose answer that is accepted among so many people, "I'm not that religious." Fortunately, there is no natural course to events.

Divine Providence took an unwelcome form: a failing mark on a whole battery of tests. True, I had not prepared for the tests at all; they counted for nothing as long as you passed them and, never having failed a test in my life, I never dreamed that I could. The head of my department suggested, ever so tactfully, that I should perhaps leave the Honors Program. Rather than submit to such mortification, I changed departments.

In the end I did well enough in both my old and my new subjects; but, at first, my graduate department had its doubts about accepting a Ph.D. candidate who had started learning the required classical languages only the previous year. They required me to demonstrate my abilities by taking high-level courses in their summer school. There went my planned trip bicycling around Europe. I showed up in Cambridge, Massachusetts (across the Charles River from Boston) on time, rented a small furnished apartment and, when Shabbos approached, I called up the Harvard Hillel House to find out when services would be.

Had I arrived as planned in the fall, I would have been greeted by three congregations—Orthodox, Conservative and Reform—and would surely have chosen the stream to which I already belonged. In the summer, however, none but the Orthodox maintained a Shabbos *minyan*. The secretary who answered the phone simply gave me a time and place, and I arrived at a *minyan* full of something I had never seen before—Jews more knowledgeable about Judaism than I was. Slowly I began learning new parts of the service, and even asking some questions I had always thought that you weren't supposed to ask. Often the answer was, "Yes, the Gemara asks that same question and...."

Little by little, I started learning. On *Tisha b'Av*, I heard *Eichah*, the *Book of Lamentations*,— for the first time in my life—a very moving chant, and a very moving text to somebody exposed daily to ghastly Vietnam War photographs. That afternoon, I put on *tefillin* for the first time since I had been thirteen years old. What would have happened had I arrived in the fall instead? In Heaven, of course, that calculation had already been made, when those exam results nudged me into this place "early."

There was a lot to learn, so I got started. I took out the tiny pocket *Chumash* with Rashi I got for my Bar Mitzvah and started slogging away at the peculiarly shaped letters and the unfamiliar style. At the rate of one *aliyah* a day, I got through it in a year. Just then a new friend arrived who was interested in *Mishnah Yomi*, a program to learn *Mishnayos* daily. Each day, rain or shine, sleet or snow, we would meet and struggle with two *Mishnayos*: first I would read the Mishnah and the commentary of Kehati, while he looked up the hard words in a dictionary; then we would switch. Each year we would make a mighty *siyum* worthy of a small yeshiva. It was not in-depth learning, but slowly the world of Torah opened before me.

As my third year began, Rav Mayer Horowitz, son of the Bostoner Rebbe, *Shlita*, founded Yeshivas Machseke Torah in nearby Brookline, peopled by college students learning on Sundays and in the evenings. The foreign language didn't bother me; I was, after all, a graduate student of Greek and Latin, and my Hebrew was better still. Nor was it difficult to read a text "in depth"; that was my career. The big problem was appreciating the depth of an answer.

For example, I did not hesitate to disagree with Rashi, as great as he was. "Rashi was human," said I. "He could make mistakes, too." Ever patient, Rav Avrohom Hirschhoff was equal to the challenge. "That's perfectly true," he once said to me. "Perhaps you are right and Rashi is wrong. On the other hand, when Rashi wrote this comment, he had learned the *entire* Talmud many times, whereas you have been learning this Gemara for only half an hour! At the moment, the chances are that Rashi is right and that you are wrong. Keep on learning, and if you are right, maybe you will eventually be able to prove it to us." Rashi was right, of course; but I had learned a lesson in how to balance the argumentative streak, that had so delighted my grandfather, with an appreciation of the great minds of the past. I too was bound by the exigencies of facts and proof. I still don't hesitate to question Rashi, but years of experience have richly borne out Rav Hirschhoff's judgment. Generally, perhaps always, Rashi will be right.

The truth of the matter is that it was not realistic to make a real yeshiva out of graduate students. Hardly any of us lived in Boston and, if we really had become serious enough to learn full-time, we would have left both the university and Boston. Back then, fortunately, no one realized that, so we learned as if we were budding yeshiva *bochurim* rather than after-school adult-education students.

When eventually I wanted my own *Shas*, I offered my father's cousin Gershon a trade: give me my grandfather's *Shas*, and I will buy you a brand-new one. Gershon wouldn't hear of it. On the spot, he packed the *Shas* into cartons and gave it all to me, refusing to take anything in return. "I am sure," he said, "that your grandfather would be delighted to know he has a grandson who can learn *Shas*, and he would want you to have it." He wouldn't take anything from my father, either.

My parents were not unhappy with my increasing religiosity. It seemed somewhat exaggerated to them, but they were not unhappy about the general direction. They had taught me to take Judaism seriously, so if I was going to extremes, it was at least to extremes on their side.

In many respects, Bnei Brak, Israel, where I settled after graduation, is a college town of the yeshiva world. Intellectualization affects every field of life, and it has the tenacity and extremism of political and religious opinions, and the centrality of the institutions of learning, that had characterized Cambridge. In Bnei Brak, learning after-hours was taken for granted. Indeed, once the electricity was finally connected in my apartment, there was hardly anything else to do in the evening. If I wanted to consider myself an intellectual, I was obviously going to have to do something more serious than two *mishnayos* a day. Yeshivos for baalei teshuvah were still rare, and I was no longer such a beginner either; but people were helpful.

My local Rav, Rav Nosson Zvi Friedmann, *zt"l*, (to whom I owe a debt greater than I can ever repay) helped; his son helped; and those who could not help had suggestions about those who could. I started learning with study partners, finding time for kollel, and learning through the *Shas* with the *Daf HaYomi* program. I did not become, and presumably never will become, one of the great scholars of the town. Bnei Brak, *Baruch Hashem*, has scholars so good that no part-timer could ever hope to challenge them. But when my parents came to visit, one rav made a point of saying to my father, "You'll be very proud of your son one day."

"I'm *already* very proud of my son," he answered.

My father's last years were not easy ones. Parkinson's disease made every movement more cumbersome; and he had to become more of a follower and less of an initiator. Finally, we received a phone call that my father was critically ill, unconscious and on a respirator, and that my sister and I should come quickly to make the necessary decisions about his medical care.

This time I knew what to pray for. I prayed that he be allowed to put on *tefillin* again, something he had not done for almost fifty years. I had never been willing or able to make any religious demands on him, beyond those of normal courtesy, but I knew that I could count on my father's scrupulous honesty. It was some weeks before he returned to consciousness, and some months before he could make decisions again, but eventually I told him the truth. "When you were sick, I prayed for your recovery; and I promised that, if you recovered, you would put on *tefillin* again. You've always stood behind me whenever I needed you. Now, please stand behind my promise and put on your *tefillin*." He did not disappoint me. The movements were difficult for him and he needed help, but he put them on. It was not the last time, either.

When people ask me why I became religious, my answer depends upon what I think they are asking. Sometimes I say, "Because it's true," which is correct. Sometimes I say, "Because I couldn't maintain the pretense of keeping part of the Torah when I wasn't keeping the rest," which is also correct. Most of the time I say, "Because my parents brought me up to be a good Jew, and taught me that being a good Jew meant keeping the Torah and mitzvos. They may not have known much Torah themselves but, as I learned what the Torah demanded of a Jew, there was really no question about which decision I should take."

I am my father's son. He worked hard on our Jewish education, and my mother always supported him. Whatever his own shortcomings in observance, shortcomings that he shared with an entire generation whose religious upbringing was rarely successful, he succeeded in passing on to his children a spark hot enough, and fuel sturdy enough, to keep the flame alive.

Becoming Me

My very earliest thoughts, the very first I can remember, were about death and eternity and where I fit into all of it. I would lie there in my bed—I was only three or maybe four—and I would imagine the world spinning like a globe and try to fit myself into the picture. What was I? Where did I fit in? Maybe it was a premature existential crisis, or maybe I was simply closer to the beginning of things. Where had I come from?

I was always attracted to Jewishness. My parents, children of European immigrants, were atypical of their upwardly mobile, suburban and assimilated generation. As is often said about Israelis, the shul they *didn't* go to—or went to only occasionally—had to be the "real" thing (Orthodox). Now that I am myself a grandmother, I also remember that grandparents have a very important role. Though my father's family ceased to be *shomer Shabbos* when he was a boy, he remembered the breaking points all too well. I heard all about the crying when the women of the family first uncovered their hair.

Anyhow, Father lived in a house with his Bubbies (grandmothers), who were *shomer Shabbos*, until they died. As a matter of fact, he used to walk them to shul on Shabbos—although his siblings accused him of simply trying to worm out of work in the family store. Years later, this translated to my own upbringing which had a certain sense of *kashrus* conscience about it all. We always had a special Friday night dinner, with *Kiddush* and pre-sliced *challah*. Now and then my father would even inexplicably say something like, "Don't sew today—it's Shabbos." Unlike most of my friends and acquaintances (all Jewish), I actually knew when I was eating *treif*, and I knew that I *should* be in shul on Yom Tov—although I wasn't.

I didn't really do anything with these feelings, except to try and dismember them the way secular society expected me to. I recall being at summer camp and eating Spam for the first time. And there it was, a process of barrier breaking: initial twangs of conscience, and then cheers—real cheers—and congratulations from my bunkmates and counselors. I then recognized a peculiar internal process which, although I did not know it then, would eventually rein me back in and fuel my ability to become *frum*. I still had some internal feelings of right and wrong, of good and bad. Every time I crossed a barrier, I felt that there was no turning back; I was irrevocably changed. Just as important, once that barrier of wrong was crossed, I felt that I would never again be in control of that area of my life again.

Guilt-free Spam led to guilt-free butterfly shrimp wrapped in bacon, and the rest was *treif*-eating history, although I always had a residual hang-up about cheeseburgers. I remember my college cafeteria served up a cauldron of melted Velveeta cheddar processed cheese to ladle onto the hamburgers. With every ladle—every delicious ladle—there I was, a bright, attractive, achieved, social and "hip" college girl of the 70s telling myself: "You are doing the wrong thing. You are doing the wrong thing."

Oy! Those points of *bechira* (free choice) are so primal. From our birth we seem to know what is wrong. I remember when my first daughter was a toddler and she sat in front of the bookshelves, not just emptying them, but tossing the books rather wildly over her shoulder. She kept looking back at me saying, "No! No! No!" These days she tells me that her toddler does the same thing, wagging her finger and saying "No!" as she climbs into her father's chair and attacks the computer keyboard.

None of this conscience mongering would ever have translated into much without the intervention and orchestration of Heaven. All that remained were my existential questions and a slight obsession with death. If this was all there was, what form should my life take? By college time, I had learned to deal with that question in a college-appropriate manner: nihilism. If this life was all there was, well, I would work hard and play harder. It is, unfortunately, all too easy to squelch a nagging *neshama*. Secular culture gives you poetry, literature and music. I had just turned twenty. My fun, my schoolwork, my art and literature and my boyfriends were all that I thought about. I can't say that I was happy, but I did try to feed my strong inner life, and the arts can make some good inroads there.

If I stood in a crowd, at some college party, could you have projected forward to see the woman I am now? Is it an accident that my best friend from college also became *frum*, years later, when she had to deal with her child's chronic genetic disease? There's no special look, there's no single special type of sensitivity. Yet, unknown to me, I was really a *frum* person waiting to happen—and, I suppose, so was my friend.

Then I met a guy I really liked, and we saw each other every day for a week. On the sixth day, however, he said that he couldn't see me that night because he was, as he awkwardly put it, a "Sabbath-observing Jew." Well, I thought that was the funniest thing I'd ever heard, although by then I at least knew what a Sabbath-observing Jew was. My older brother had been *frum* for many years; but this fellow did not act like my brother. Perhaps he was afraid I would run in the opposite direction at the mention of the word religion. Well, I ran in the same direction as he. Suddenly I was freed up. I was in a safe zone. The two of us created our own social context; and although where it would lead wasn't clear, I now could explore my Judaism too.

I don't think he had ever thought much about the existence of Hashem. We spent the early months of our relationship arguing out that possibility and then, I guess, I realized that I had always believed in Hashem and needed no proof. My boyfriend, and future husband, was working at the time with someone who eventually put us in touch with the Bostoner Rebbe. The Rebbe's approach was slow and easy, both for us and for our parents, who had lots of their own issues as well. When I talk about all this, the mechanics don't interest me as much as the internal process. It was the Rebbe who had to engineer all the mechanics. It must have been quite a job!

I will have to summarize the next part. Some very deep and personal issues came up here, and these are best kept personal. That's part of the privacy and restraint that all polite people owe each other. Still, I'd like to mention a few points of satisfaction that impressed me as I learned more about what I was getting into. First, here was society where women had dignity and weren't viewed solely through the lens of sexuality. I didn't care anything about the women's movement, although I was studying in a first-rate women's college. I knew, mostly from vast dating experience, that men and women were absolutely different and had different life roles to play. I think that back then I could have scooped John Grey and written my own Mars/Venus treatise. Second, I learned that I could indeed live a life which was full of meaning, even though it was headed towards death (the answer to my childhood conundrum). Third, I learned that I could say "no" to myself, stick with it and have everything to gain.

The Rebbe's way continued to be slow and easy. We still weren't experienced in saying "no" to ourselves. We also had lots of problems with the outside world, including our parents; but the Rebbe continued to guide us—until this day.

I also have to admit to a few strange reversals along the way. Even by age twenty, I hadn't once thought about having children. My not-*frum* self would probably never have had children. Figure that one out! Still, my first reaction to many *frum* experiences was often intensely negative, contrasting strongly with my later more positive reaction. For example, I once saw, at a small women's *shalosh seudos*, a woman sitting to the side nursing her baby; my reaction was so intense that I actually thought I would throw up. A couple of years later, I was that woman. Similarly, the first time I sat at a separate all-women Shabbos table, I was very angry. Although I knew that was only because the friend I had come with was male, I still felt awkward.

As I get older, I constantly evaluate how I'm doing and how I did it. The Rebbe was the single largest factor. Then there was the combination of my search for self-preservation, female dignity and psychological *tikkun* (repair). What I had been missing was the self-esteem that comes from being a *tzelem Elokim*. Once I put my *bechira* points in another system, I gained a lot more control over my life. Realizing that Hashem controls this world (and the next), took a lot of psychological, emotional and philosophical burden off myself.

On one hand, I've changed entirely; on the other hand, I haven't changed at all. That is the beauty of the Rebbe's approach. The first time I was *frum* in shul on Yom Kippur and really took it seriously,

I looked around me and thought: Why are all these people praying? What do they have to *daven* for? They're already *frum*. Sometimes I can't believe how innocent I was.

Sometimes I have a tremendous chip on my shoulder about not having had the advantage of being shaped by an early Torah education. Sometimes I'm grateful for the strength I had to muster to grow when I broke out of the starting gate. A few years out of college, I was a full-fledged *balabusta* with a couple of babies, community responsibility and a Rebbetzin of sorts to neophytes a year or two behind me. I hope at one hundred and twenty years, those *zechusim* will outweigh my many shortcomings. I can now accept both as part of my becoming me.

TIKKUN OLAM

No one comes to Torah as a blank slate, and my dramatic spiritual growth at age fourteen had its roots in my early childhood. I grew up in a city of about 100,000 in Pennsylvania. Our town had a synagogue for each of the three "denominations," and our neighborhood was the main Jewish area at the time. All the schools—from kindergarten through Albright College—were located on our street. Two paternal uncles and an aunt all lived on our block, and several cousins lived on the next block. On Sunday mornings, the family would all gather at the home of Aunt Sara, a quiet gentle woman who used to walk downtown, rather than take a bus or trolley. She apparently closely resembled her mother, Riva. Grandmother Riva died early of cancer and

Grandfather Yaakov, an itinerant rural tailor, died in Europe; so I never really knew either of my religious paternal grandparents.

These Sunday morning gatherings were a retreat from the family's non-Jewish weekday contacts, a return to their Yiddish-speaking European childhood. They came from a crossroads, not even a *shtetel*, with just three or four Jewish families and a dozen or so non-Jewish ones, near Vilna. Their origins were Chassidic, probably Chabad, according to Uncle Lou, the oldest brother, who still subscribed to a Yiddish newspaper, was successful in business and proudly drove a Packard. Their memories and childhood had little to do with me, a young American boy who did not understand Yiddish, but who, to their surprise, wanted to be there to absorb a bit of their Jewish ambience. Aunt Sadie's married children and their families also came by. One of her sons had intermarried, but his wife was warmly "adopted" by the family. Another son intermarried and disappeared, completely cutting himself off from his family.

My father himself was rather withdrawn from our own family, although quite at home with his siblings. He rarely said anything about his own childhood, which was apparently pretty horrible. In Lithuania, he had lacked food and was surrounded by corpses in World War I. He had also lived in a different inner world from us, wearing *peyos*, and traveling with his family to nearby townlets to spend the holidays with a *minyan*. Perhaps, when I later adopted Orthodoxy, I was seeking to reconnect with his lost world, although my intellectualized *Misnagdishe* yeshiva was actually a far cry from his simple *Chassidishe* upbringing.

Though rather weak, American Judaism had the usual public institutions in my hometown: schools, shuls and an active, but not very Jewish, community center. My beginnings were not auspicious. I failed first grade (although I was outstanding thereafter) and was an individualistic, creative rebel from a very early age, possibly a result of my father's "laid-back" attitude to his unfamiliar American children. I was not sent to Hebrew school until age ten; and then our

Conservative shul's school was really the only possible choice. The local Reform temple was very *goyish*, anti-Zionist and served pork. The Orthodox synagogue was basically for older, Yiddish-speaking immigrants (although their president had intermarried, while the head of the traditionalist Conservative shul was *shomer Shabbos!*).

Our school was fine in its way, giving us all the Jewish education and enthusiasm they could, without turning us off by undue religious pressure. In the beginning, the teachers met us in a taxi after public school, and stopped on the way to Hebrew school to buy us ice cream (very effective!). We were taught Hebrew, *Siddur, Chumash*, etc., several afternoons and Sunday mornings, with programs and films about Zionism and Israel, giving us pride in being Jewish, albeit non-observant.

I was, alas, a strong advocate of non-kosher "deli" in our Jewish scout troop, although our family bought meat only from the local kosher butcher. The wonderful aromas of the local Jewish delicatessen also gave Judaism a good smell. I enjoyed the junior congregation services on Shabbos mornings, run by the kids—but then I would often go to the double-feature at the local cinema, not sensing any contradiction. Although my own best friends were not Jewish (my school Valentine girl was Scandinavian!), I also felt part of the Jewish *chevra*. I was friendly with the rabbi's kids, although I urged them to do everything as usual on Yom Tov! I was also in all sorts of "businesses" from about age eight, and often treated myself to a daily movie. When everyone else bought Schwinn bikes, I bought a magnificent Columbia bike from a brochure. Perhaps a certain lack of conformity may have been necessary for someone in such an assimilated environment to become Orthodox. In any case, my early life was full, but contradictory.

I particularly remember one Hebrew school play about the Baal Shem Tov taking his disciples on a hayride throughout the night, while we, the disciples, sang a beautiful Chassidic niggun, chanting *di-di, di-di, di-di-di-didei.* The goal of the nocturnal journey was to meet a saintly elderly couple, possibly ignorant and illiterate, whose souls and hearts overflowed with love of Hashem and their fellow human beings. It struck me as so beautiful that it remained with me for life (possibly connected to thoughts of my grandparents).

While we kids did not relate to most of the rabbis, who were not particularly emotional or child-like, we all loved the old European *shamashim* and the Bar Mitzvah teacher, who both exuded warmth and deep, simple piety. After Bar Mitzvah, most of us left Jewish learning and observance, although I at least retained fond memories of school.

My mother's three brothers, all highly intellectual non-observant liberals, often gave me sophisticated books to read; but my fondest childhood memories are of her warm and loving parents, who ran a mom-and-pop grocery store in New Jersey. They were loved even by their non-Jewish customers, to whom they extended both credit and friendship. My grandmother was the stronger of the two. She remained Orthodox, would not work on Shabbos, and tried to keep me from eating non-kosher food. Although she would brook no discrimination against any human being, she was quite broken by the marriage of her son to a non-Jew. My grandfather was a modern "humanistic" Jew, very involved with the *Tanach* and human decency, but not observant. He came to the States before his wife and saw much more of the country. His own mother, a Yiddish poetess, was blind but alert, and lived until her late 90s.

We cousins lived at the base of a mountain and frequently hiked and biked it, building hideouts in the woods, and so on. In the winter, the city blocked off the hilly streets during snowstorms, and we spent many, many hours in high-speed sledding down the hills. Such joys of life and nature may have been another positive pre-set trigger for my later enthusiasm for the world's Creator. How different from an Orthodox big-city upbringing, where kids pore over Talmud and Shul*chan Aruch* for endless hours!

So, perhaps, I was ready to get closer to my grandparent's world and Orthodoxy. Ready or not, around age fourteen, I met Rabbi Chaim Seiger, originally from Cleveland, who had *smichah* from Rav Henoch Leibowitz's Yeshivas Chofetz Chayim in Williamsburg, an intensely Jewish neighborhood in New York City. He took over our town's old-fashioned and dying Shomrei Habrith synagogue, in the old immigrant Jewish neighborhood near our town's extensive railway yards. I often passed it on my bike while going to pick up ten books at a time from the local library. (I had become a voracious early reader, also a good preparation for a book-oriented, Orthodox life.)

Since there were no young people left in the shul, Rabbi Seiger took the initiative and rounded up all the fourteen-year-old Jewish kids he could find. One day I bicycled past my house and saw this snazzily dressed man talking to my mother on the porch. Since I was then in the stamp business, I feared that he might be a postal inspector, so I kept on going. I later found out that he was a rabbi, who wanted us post-Bar Mitzvah kids to come and study with him a few hours a week. It was pretty much the *last* thing I felt like doing, but my mother was really adamant. The rabbi had warned her of the great dangers of assimilation and intermarriage in a weak Jewish community like ours. At the time, I already had a lovely, bright non-Jewish girlfriend. In fact, one of my most joyous moments came when I, the Jewish intellectual "star student" of the class, beat up the non-Jewish student who attacked me for taking one of "their" girls.

Highly reluctant, I went off to Rabbi Seiger's classes with five or ten other Jewish boys and girls. To my surprise, he and his wife, *a"h*, were the most stimulating and alive people I had ever met. Gradually, his explanations of Judaism began to take hold and

I started walking the long distance to his shul several times each Shabbos. I developed a fondness for the old Yiddish-speaking men who made up the *minyan* (when they were short, they called in a few "boys" from the local Jewish detention center!). I felt a special beauty in the atmosphere and songs of the third meal on Shabbos, a carryover from Europe, even though the old-timers were often no longer observant and their children had intermarried.

When I was about fifteen, Rabbi Seiger organized a trip to New York for us, which opened our eyes to a truly Orthodox Jewish world, one we had never experienced. My closest friend, Mel, and I gradually became quite observant. Family friends suggested that my parents take me to a psychologist!

By then, I had already concluded that the typical American "worship" of group sports was a nonsensical waste of time and energy, and started studying with Rav Seiger. The adage of R. Yehuda ben Tama in *Pirkei Avos* that fifteen is the right age for Talmud study certainly fit me. I could not follow its abstract logic at fourteen, but it suddenly clicked a year later (Mel had grasped it earlier).

Rabbi Seiger soon decided that complete immersion in an authentic yeshiva world would benefit both Mel and I. So he convinced our parents to let us spend two weeks, during the summer, at Yeshivas Chofetz Chayim, his own rigorous Slobodka-based *mussar* yeshiva. At the time, there were almost no systematic beginner yeshivas, like Ohr Samayach and Aish HaTorah today. So we just plunged into that advanced yeshiva, with some help from the kind students and teachers. I had been eating only peanut butter and lettuce sandwiches at high school (about all I concluded was kosher there) so it was quite pleasant to be, for the first time in my life, at a school where everything was kosher. Shlomo Weiss' great bakery was also nearby. Mel and I both took to the yeshiva like ducks to the water, and we bought ourselves wide-brimmed black hats to fit into our new environment. After the two weeks, we both wanted to quit high school and go off to Williamsburg to learn Torah full-time. My father characteristically "O.K.-ed" it, although he predicted that I would soon tire of this updated version of the world he had left and come back home.

My cousin, who drove me to yeshiva in New York, more bluntly told me that I was just escaping from an "unhappy home environment." But I argued strongly with him and even got him to read the *Kitzur Shulchan Aruch* in English. He found parts of it extraordinarily beautiful and inspiring, and other parts "petty and backward" (e.g., the order of putting on and tying one's shoes). In any case, I never came back. I remained Orthodox the rest of my life, albeit with lingering doubts and questions. I never fully understood or adopted today's *yeshivishe* attitude.

In short, after three years of initial ecstasy in this new world of holiness, intellect and warm camaraderie, for which I am truly grateful, I began to doubt the advisability of my colleagues' way of life. They were all fine people, but the idea of spending all day studying and single until thirty gradually lost its appeal for me. Still, despite my new doubts, I never once stopped my observance. My reason was typically intellectualized: I lost nothing by observing, but I could wreck my life, both in this world and the next, by not observing! Two books eventually encouraged my faith—Yehuda Halevi's *Kuzari* and Isidore Epstein's *Judaism*—and I gained a stronger belief than ever before.

I began attending Brooklyn College at night, and supported myself by teaching first-grade secular subjects in a Chassidic *cheder*. I just barely managed to support my grand old 1950 Packard, myself and a freezing rented top-floor room near Coney Island. I would turn on the oven and open the door towards my bed every morning, because the landlord paid for the gas!

I had previously heard about Yeshiva University—part yeshiva, part university, with dorms—and it seemed an ideal combination. Although the *yeshivishe* world sometimes depicted it as a den of iniquity, I finally decided to apply, assuming that my *mussar* training would, at worst, enable me to reform it! I was accepted with a full scholarship and attended it from February 1959 until my graduation in 1961. While everyone else complained, I was in heaven, living in a decent dorm with fabulous food. I liked the combination of yeshiva and secular studies, the warm intelligent faculty and the pleasant *chaverim*. Blending Torah study and *derech eretz* (worldly ways) struck me as a stimulating and inspiring way of life. While I found the prevailing slander of Y.U. to be grossly exaggerated, I did contribute to its religious atmosphere by becoming the founding editor of its newspaper, *Hamodea*.

I majored in math and did well at it; but my heart was not really in such abstract preoccupations. Psychology seemed impractical; so I applied to law schools. Rejected by Yale, where Alan Dershowitz taught Law and Psychology, I got a scholarship from Harvard, through which Hashem brought me to Boston. In Cambridge, my roommate and I lived in the home of a lovely old religious lady. Originally from Europe, she distrusted anything not from her childhood. We mounted a constant campaign to get her to try such new-fangled things as bananas!

Besides attending Harvard Law School, a wonderful place, I taught Hebrew school, inspiring myself as I tried to inspire my young charges. I soon discovered two wonderful Jewish resources. Rav Joseph Ber Soloveitchik *zt"l*, inspired about 400 people, from all over New England, every Saturday night, with his brilliant Torah lectures. A much smaller number attended his Sunday morning Talmud classes, which also appealed to me less.

The New England Chassidic Center, headed by the Bostoner Rebbe, Rav Levi Yitzchak Horowitz, *shlita*, reached out to both religious and non-religious students in every way. I greatly enjoyed the Rebbe's joyous energy and humanism. I was also set up for many inspiring Shabbos meals by them, and by Erwin Katz of the nearby Young Israel Synagogue. Years later, I would sometimes leave Rav Soloveitchik's Shabbos afternoon question-and-answer session to be spiritually refreshed by the warm, lively third Shabbos meal by the Bostoner Rebbe.

During my last year of law school, I married and began my real estate business by buying a three-family house in Cambridge (I myself lived in much cheaper Somerville). I also opened a small store at home. After graduation, I briefly held a legal position in the trial department of a local law firm, but didn't really like the work. I began buying more houses, borrowing the down-payments via second mortgages, and so on. I also continued writing for the local papers, and studying Torah. I became an ardent believer in Modern Orthodoxy and Religious Zionism, although I continued to be moved by both the warm prayers of the Bostoner Rebbe and the quiet refinement of the Twersky family and the Tolna Shul (especially the old Rebbetzin, who became central to the *shteibel*, after the Tolna Rebbe suffered a serious stroke).

In 1969, I visited Israel and was gripped by the reality of the imminent redemption. While determined to move there, I put it off for five years, to my later regret. In 1974, I finally retired and came to Israel, where I and my children, grandchildren and great-grandchild all live to this day, *Baruch Hashem*. Here, I helped restore the almost abandoned Bet Yisroel Shul in Yemin Moshe, which was slated for renovation as a community center. I started a lecture series there and taught for some years at Machon Meir and the Israel Center. Finally, some years ago, I created the Torah Outreach Program (TOP) and started publishing an electronic *parsha* newsletter. I have expanded my knowledge, both religious and secular, and try to write about the relationship between Hashem's Torah and His world. When I knew little, I had a clear-cut, black-and-white picture of things and a great sense of my ability to accomplish anything. Now, older and hopefully wiser, I sense how little power I have to change anything. Ultimately, we are all in Hashem's Hands. Although He remains inscrutable, He wants us to be his partners in *tikkun olam*, perfecting the world.

It's a long way from Pennsylvania, and what's ahead, as I plunge forward down life's one-way street, only He knows.

THE SMILE

I t was my senior year of high school, and I was becoming a baal teshuva. This may seem unusual, since my family was religious and I had been in various yeshiva day schools and high schools all my life; but—truth be told—my experiences there had been horrible from a spiritual point of view. I wanted to go to college as far away from there as possible, but, unfortunately, "there" was New York, the center of Torah Judaism in the United States. Where else could a nominally *frum* teenager go? Then I heard about a sympathetic, modern, very special Chassidic Rebbe who lived in Boston. Maybe there were alternatives to New York after all! I applied to Boston University and was accepted. Then I went to Boston for an exploratory Shabbos to look around and meet the Rebbe.

I had never *davened* in a Chassidic *shteibel* before. While there were a few *shtreimels* and *bekeshes*, most of the people there looked very much like me, although, admittedly, my hair was longer than most. Then the Rebbe came in. The room lit up! I had never seen a man like him before. There was something special about him, although I was still very ambivalent. I was deciding the next four years of my life based on a man I didn't even know. Worse, he didn't look all that approachable.

Then the Rebbe began to speak. From the looks of him, I had expected a broken half-English, half-Yiddish *dvar Torah*, brimming with deep intellect and complex interpretations of some abstruse aspect of Torah law. What came out was a Boston accent and a humorous story, which I soon forgot, and a smile, which I will never forget. It was a warm, tender and inviting smile. A smile that later greeted me at his *tish* and at our first private discussion that Shabbos. That smile made me a Bostoner Chassid.

• • •

After one year at Boston University, and two years as a baal teshuva, the Rebbe advised me to leave Boston and study in Israel. The temptations I was facing at the university, and not always overcoming, were not in the best interests of my Torah growth. The Rebbe helped me choose a yeshiva, and I stayed in touch with him during my two years abroad.

Soon after I returned, I met the woman who later became my wife. During many weeks of trying to decide whether to propose or not—with major bouts of cold feet in between—I told her that it would mean a lot to me if we could go to Boston, meet the Rebbe and get his advice and *brachah*. My wife-to-be, who came from a solid Modern Orthodox, Young Israel background, had never had anything to do with a Rebbe before. She wasn't exactly thrilled by my idea; but, to humor me (and warm my cold feet), she agreed to join me in Boston for a Shabbos.

The whole scene was totally foreign to her. At the Friday night meal, the men sat with other men and the Rebbe, while the women sat behind a *mechitza* with the Rebbetzin. She couldn't even sit next to me! Stuck, she sat down next to the Rebbetzin, her back to the Rebbe, with great trepidation.

Then something happened that spoke volumes about the Rebbe's sensitivity and insight. He called over one of his *gabbaim* and whispered something in his ear. The *gabbai* went over to the Rebbetzin and whispered something in her ear. The Rebbetzin asked the young woman to her left to switch places with my girlfriend so she could face the Rebbe's table and see me and the Rebbe. Without ever having spoken to her, the Rebbe sensed that she was uncomfortable, and that this small gesture would make her Shabbos more meaningful.

The next morning, after shul, the Rebbe asked to see us. Well, not exactly "us".... First he wanted to see my girlfriend on her own. That was all I needed! She walked into the Rebbe's study with the most frightened look on her face. She gave me eyes that could kill, silently complaining "What are you making me do now!"

She came out close to an hour later...white as a ghost. All she said was "The Rebbe wants to see you now." I walked into the study. Rebbe was sitting in his big chair, leaning back, with another big, special smile on his face...giving me a thumbs up sign! He said, "I'm ready to make your *l'chayim* at *Shalosh Seudas* today! I honestly expected some West Side Manhattan Jewish American Princess, but she is a gem! Don't lose her! Make the *l'chayim* (the first step towards engagement) today!" I was totally taken aback!

"Slow down, Rebbe" I said. "We only came for your guidance and a *brachah*...I'm not ready to do it *today!*" So the Rebbe gave us his *brachah* and we were engaged a few weeks later.

• • •

One more "smile" story. During my single years, I had lived in Riverdale, New York, a very modern, upscale community. It wasn't the kind of place where you saw Chassidim walking down the street. I once asked my shul rabbi if he would like me to invite the Bostoner Rebbe to address the congregation some weekday night. He gratefully accepted my suggestion, and we organized the event.

The room was packed with all kinds of different people, from all kinds of different backgrounds. The only element that was definitely not present was *Chassidish*. The shul Rabbi got up to introduce the Rebbe. The audience was totally quiet as he got up to speak. The Rebbe walked up to the podium, dressed in his long black coat and wide-brimmed black hat, stroking his long graying beard. In short, he and his stylish, upwardly mobile audience seemed worlds apart.

Once in place, the Rebbe slowly began his speech...in Yiddish! The audience began to mumble. As he spoke, the mumbling grew louder and louder. This was Riverdale...young, modern Riverdale. Most of the congregants didn't even know Yiddish. The mumbles soon turned into loud whispers. The Rebbe stopped talking...took a pregnant pause, and then, in his Bostonian English accent, said... "Fooled you!" What a great icebreaker! The Rebbe's address was a huge success.

THE TURNING POINT

It never was clear to me the exact moment or place at which my life's journey first veered at a definitive crossroads and turning point—at least not at the beginning. My religious life developed slowly, day by day, although it did reach a dramatic decision point later on. I had had a solid "traditional" upbringing, but I knew that I was looking for something more.

I grew up in London. Although we lived outside of London's Jewish Golders Green/Hendon neighborhood, my family, the local shul and our community were, at the very least, quite traditional. Then, of course, there were also those girls who knew "more." They seemed to know what they were doing and to feel more at home in their *Yiddishkeit*. They had parents and grandparents who seemed to set the rules for them and who later would arrange their *shidduchim* for them. I, by contrast, felt very much alone. I didn't have family connections in the *frum* world that was gradually becoming more and more important to me. I didn't have brothers who went to yeshiva. I always felt different. In contrast to the typical Jewish American immigrant, who tried his best to speak an unaccented English and to forget that he ever came from Poland, I dearly wished that my parents, z"l, had European accents, just like those of my friends. Their parents all seemed to be *heimish, balabatish* Holocaust survivors.

I went to an all-girls high school where, although it was not a Jewish school, around half of the student body was Jewish. A large proportion of the Jewish girls were religiously observant, and we even had separate Jewish prayers. When we gave presentations in French literature, it fell to me to explain how Hashem could know the future and still allow us free choice. And what of the debate on Shakespeare's *Merchant of Venice*? Was Shakespeare unfair in his portrayal of Jews? Was Shylock really so rotten after all?

Although this was not a particularly nurturing situation religiously, I was becoming ever more religious—in typical English style. It wasn't a question of black and white. I wasn't suddenly leaving my family home. I didn't need to leave. My mother was quite happy to serve food with any *hechsher* I wanted, to keep separate tablecloths for milk and meat, even to order *Cholov Yisroel*, and so on. I had no crusades to fight or confrontations to instigate. Instead, I needed to find a certain missing quality in my life. It was more a question of searching for a place that would give me a sense of meaning and belonging. At home and in school, socially, I never really felt I could be myself.

One day, at a religious social gathering, someone ever-so-discreetly pointed out a certain boy wearing a dark suit and hat. "See that boy over there. He's actually a baal teshuva; his family is not *frum.*" Just what was that supposed to mean? Was he a second-class citizen? Had I just been privy to some damaging evidence that could later be held against him? I unconsciously decided that I, thereafter, had to learn all that I could, without publicizing the fact that I was hearing certain things for the first time.

Of course, all of this placed me very firmly in no man's land. London in the '70s was a rather closed society. I knew few other Jewish "outsiders" living in London, and Shabbos did not come with ready open-house invitations as they do in Jerusalem. No religious family invited me to experience Shabbos with them; after all, wasn't I "one of them" anyway?

Today, in a sense, it is easier, more clear. A student shows up in Israel from the States with no idea of who Hashem is or what Shabbos is. She arrives at the Wall, is welcomed with open arms, and realizes how meaningless and empty her life has been until now. She starts all over, and her every baby-step is greeted with loving support and encouragement. That's Jerusalem, as I've been privileged to know it for the last twenty-five years, and somehow, subconsciously, I knew I had to get there, although I had no idea of how.

After high school, the "in thing" was to spend a year in Israel, having deferred one's university admissions for a year. During all my years of school, since I could first remember, scholastic achievement had been all-important, particularly in my high school, which was considered high-class and of high academic standards. Continuing on to university was a given and the general atmosphere that permeated the school was competitive and—dare I say it—almost cutthroat. Some of the teachers, elderly English spinsters, both felt and made it known to their young charges that poor marks or unsatisfactory scholastic performance were the marks of a poor, unsatisfactory person. You *were* your marks.

Nothing and nobody outside of that was really worth anything. Not few were the occasions when a teacher verbally demolished a pupil for lack of attention in class, not doing homework, etc.—all were cardinal sins. I kept the rules, wore my uniform, walked on the right side of the stairs and didn't bring oranges to school unpeeled. I did everything right. I even got accepted into a good university to study French...and yet something was missing.

I could have done all of this, spent a year in Israel, come back to study, and ended up teaching French in the Jewish girls' school. I could have continued becoming increasingly religious and done all those things. Yet, I had an increasing urge to find a place where I truly belonged, rather than just blending in like a chameleon. In retrospect, I was rather a successful chameleon, but the strain of trying to adapt and adjust was both lonely and at times demoralizing. I was tired of being on the outside.

I chose an Israeli seminary geared towards girls from *frum* homes. The teachers really cared. Many of them were Americans who had truly integrated into Yerushalmi society and were living an authentic Torah life there. It became increasingly difficult for me to picture myself leaving. Suddenly, the gray cloud that had surrounded me for so long was beginning to dissipate, and I could see the sun peeping out from behind the clouds.

The year progressed, beautiful but not without difficulties. Until now, I had struggled with each and every step forward, whether in *tznius*, *kashrus*, or Shabbos. I was not used to simply being told, "This is how it is done here." True, it was breathtakingly beautiful to literally see, feel and hear Shabbos permeate a whole neighborhood, as the Shabbos siren sounded throughout Bayit Vegan. But what of all my previous battles to succeed? Was I simply supposed to put down my secular tools, become one of the crowd, and forget about French and English literature or the political situation? Was I to lock it all up in a suitcase labeled *treif*? On the other hand, what about Shabbos? As a student, I was now officially "homeless," so I spent many an enlightening, soul-warming Shabbos with families for whom Torah was their very existence. That too could not be denied.

So the year passed, and all too soon was coming to a close. What was I going to do next? I could hardly justify four or five years studying French literature, followed by a year of teacher training, if I had no intention of living in England. French in Israel is at best a fourth language. Furthermore, one of my highly respected mentors informed me that teaching in an irreligious Israeli university was simply not an option. Moving permanently to *Eretz Yisroel* also meant leaving my mother alone in London. My father, *z"l*, had passed away when I was fourteen, and she was caring for my ailing grandmother. The housemother of the seminary suggested I ask a Rav for *daas Torah* (a Torah perspective) regarding what I should do.

The Rav listened to my story in great detail: where I was coming from, what I would do if I stayed (get a job, board with a family) and what I would do if I left. At the end of our conversation, he told me that he wanted to consider what I had said, and that I should call him back in two or three days.

It was a long two or three days. A close friend from London who was visiting in Jerusalem asked me what I would do if the Rav said "No. Return to England." This friend had been studying in Gateshead and her *hashkofos* were certainly in the right place. I was stunned by the question. I honestly did not know what I would do. Go back to the gray cloud, to not belonging, to a life that meant more sitting on the fence? And yet, without *Daas Torah*, how could I just pack my bags and leave London? It was a difficult time. I only realized how difficult when I could hear my heart thumping, as I dialed the Rav's number. My voice trembled ever so slightly, as I stammered my question and waited for the answer that would affect my entire future. I don't remember his good wishes for *hatzlocha*. All I heard was that, upon due consideration, his decision was that I should remain in *Eretz Yisroel*.

I put the phone down and somehow got back next door to the family with whom I was staying. Twenty years ago, not everyone in Jerusalem had their own phone. It was common to use a neighbor's phone. It was also common to share many other things—from Shabbos, to bags of sugar, to washing machines, to a listening ear.

I was walking on air and, at the same time, I was more than a little afraid. I was grateful for all that had brought me to this point. It was a turning point, but not because I was saying goodbye to a previous life I no longer had ties to. My past and relationship with my mother and old friends was secure. I already had a job and, for a while now, had boarded with a family. Rather it was a turning point in adding an emotionally secure future.

I felt both happy and overwhelmed. I felt both alone and that, in Jerusalem, I could never feel alone again. As I informed my university in London that I was not coming back to study, I wondered for a time what became of a person who simply works in an office.

All those years of being conditioned to believe that intellectual prowess alone makes you a worthwhile person had certainly affected my order of priorities, at least temporarily; but the pure Torah atmosphere of Jerusalem had changed all of that. I had come home to a place where warmth and authenticity came first. I had found what I had been searching for. During my seminary year I had often wondered which was real: the place I had grown up in or the magic joy of Torah that fills Jerusalem. Could I simply leave London, or was that really just running away to a dreamland?

It's now twenty-five years later, and there have been many other decisions and turning points in my life. And yet, it seems to me, as I look back, that the hardest and most meaningful decisions have involved choosing, not between black and white, but between gray and white. Yet, somehow, that very choice brings with it a feeling of coming home. *Baruch Hashem*, that's a yearning and a dream that you never have to wake up from.

Fragments From A Long Journey

And on that day the Great Shofar will sound,
And they will come, those lost in the land of Ashur,
And those rejected in the land of Egypt (Mitzraim)
And they will worship Hashem in the Holy (Temple)
Mount in Jerusalem.

- Yishayahu 27:13

For a generation lost in a land of *Ishur* (approval) where everything is permitted, or in a land of *Mitzarim* (limitations) where one's authentic spirituality is hemmed in on all sides, one needs a Great Shofar indeed to awake one from one's numbing spiritual sleep. Indeed, is it anything short of miraculous that Jews nearly "clueless" about their roots can find their way back—from an environment usually apathetic, always distracting and often deliberately misleading? And is it only coincidence that this often comes through our return to our natural environment, the worship of Hashem in Jerusalem?

THE LAST JEW IN THE FAMILY

I'm seven or eight years old playing hide-and-seek at Billy O'Brien's Halloween party. I open a door down the corridor. A shaft of light shoots in. There, hanging on the wall, above the bed, looks like somebody about my size. Uh-oh! I'm frightened. I go, sit on the sofa and wait for my big brother to come and take me, his little sister, home.

And I never tell anybody about the kid nailed to the wall in Billy's apartment.

Later, I see the same thing on a necklace. "What's that?" I ask Mom, as casually as I can, trying not to arouse her suspicion.

"That's Jesus," she says. "The lady is a Christian. Christians believe in Jesus." (Huh?)

"And are we Christians, Mummy?"

"No darling. We're Jews."

"Oh. What are Jews?"

"What? Oh," says Mom, turning back to her baking. "Jews are people who DON'T believe in Jesus."

That was my whole Jewish education.

• • •

Two years later, one of my friends is staying out of school for a holy day of some sort. "Can I stay out, too?" I ask Mom.

"What's the holiday about?" she asks.

"It celebrates learning, I think."

"Well," Mom smiles. "Do you think G-d wants you to celebrate learning by missing school?" She has a point.

I go at night instead. I slip out for some shul hopping, someplace along Beacon Street. There's singing, clapping, stomping from inside a building. Guys are pouring out into the street, holding little kids. Holding hands. Holding enormous scrolls. Dancing.

The guy in the middle is beaming and everyone's having a great time.

"Who's that?" I ask my friend, as we hurry to her temple a few blocks down.

"That's a rabbi, stupid," she says, and pulls me along after her.

I discover Saturdays, find the "temples" along Beacon Street, and try some temple hopping.

It's pretty embarrassing, because I can't read a word. When do I bend? When do I bow? When do I turn the page?

Then ... disaster. The girl next to me stands up. So I stand up. The girl hisses through clenched teeth. "Sit down! You didn't lose your father like I did. Who are you to stand up? You're not even a member of this temple!"

Oy!

That's it! Mortifying. Literally, embarrassed to death (actually a Talmudic concept).

• • •

Years later. Marriage. Divorce. College. Grad School. Paris. Back to the States.

Sunday brunch. My boy is turning eight. I have nothing to give him. His dad knows even less than I do. I pick up the phone and call Harvard Hillel.

"Is there some rabbi with a long black beard on Beacon Street?"

"No. But there's a rabbi with a long WHITE beard. Maybe you're looking for...."

I dial the number. Some guy answers. "I'm looking for a Jewish education for my little boy."

"Come right over," he says. It's the Bostoner Rebbe. I leave my friends finishing their pastries and head to Brookline.

The guy with the long once-black, now white, beard has this smile. Warm...ironic...like he shares an unspoken joke with you, that you'll remember momentarily. Or like "I've been expecting you...How have you been?"

"I'm looking for a Jewish education for my boy. My childhood friends, who went to Hebrew school, mostly married out."

"And yourself?" asks the Rebbe.

"I know there is a letter shaped like a W that makes a *shhh* sound. And I can follow along in the English, if I hear Avraham, Yitzhak and

Yaakov in the Hebrew. That's as far as I got before ..." my voice trails off. I feel so...stupid.

The Rebbe beams at me. "And where do you live?"

"Harvard Square. Cambridge. So what do you think? Maybe I should put my boy into Maimonides, the Jewish Day School?"

The Rebbe shakes his head thoughtfully, but no.

I'm shocked. Shouldn't a rabbi leap at the chance to get a kid a Jewish education?

"I'm not saying you should change your lifestyle," the Rebbe says with sincerity. "But it could be hard for the boy to go to a school that has different values than he finds at home. Why don't you both come for Shabbos?"

The old terror returns to my heart. When to bend and when to bow.... Then I look at the Rebbe, eyes full of kindness and gentle curiosity. The knot in my stomach unknots. "What time is Shabbos?"

"Shabbos is twenty-four hours. Come at 7 o'clock. You'll sleep at our house."

I come the first week. Don't understand a word. But the Rebbetzin lets me help her set the Shabbos table, and we have a good time chopping pickles. What are we laughing about? I don't know. We laugh a lot, the Rebbetzin and I.

The next week, I bring my boy.

The next week, we go to the beach.

Wednesday morning, the phone rings. "This is the Bostoner Rebbe. Where were you last Shabbos? We miss you when you're not here." And then, a humorous, "Don't make me call you again!"

The Bostoner Rebbe. He becomes my *tateh*...my *zaide*...my...I don't know...my Rebbe.

• • •

Two years later, I'm shuttling between Jerusalem and the States. Working and learning in a woman's yeshiva. Stateside, I always stop on my way to the airport, for a quick sit-down with the Rebbe.

This time, the Rebbe asks, "What's troubling you." Odd, nothing ever troubles me much. Hmmm....

"Well, there *is* one thing. I feel bad that my parents haven't met you. It would be a comforting connection for them, since I'm in Israel most of the time." The Rebbe keeps me longer than usual, that day. Chatting about Torah. Chatting about shul happenings. Just chatting...odd....

Finally, the secretary comes in. "Her father's here," she says. The Rebbe says, "Send him in." I guess he figured that my parents were taking me to the airport. Duh!

My Dad comes in. He looks at the Rebbe. He laughs. Oy!

I hang my head. Peek up. The Rebbe's laughing, too. And they're exchanging "*Shalom Aleichem*." Huh?

"What was that?" I ask Dad, as we head down the stairs. "Do you guys know each other?"

"It's rather a long story," says Dad. But that's another story.

• • •

Today. I'm a college chaplain in the States. The academic year is over, so I'm packing my bags again. Leaving next week for the wild, wild Middle East.

My little boy is getting married. My little boy, who came with me to the Rebbe's... who came with me to yeshiva. who, when the time was right, the Rebbe did send to Maimonides. Now my boy is getting married in Israel to the sweetest of the sweetest Jewish girls.

It's a funny thing, but my son's soulmate was born the very same year that I first took my boy for Shabbos at the Rebbe's.

I can't wait to tell the Rebbe.... He'll smile, that smile of a joke that we share, that we're always in the process of remembering.

My son knows when to bend and bow, and when to turn the page. He makes *Kiddush*, speaks Hebrew, knows Talmud, and reads from the Torah. My son, the doctor, the last Jew in my father's family, recently opened a bank account with his fiancé. They're saving for the Jewish education of my future grandchildren.

And as for the Rebbe, he never judged. He rarely advised. He simply welcomed us home.

TIME-LINE, LIFE-LINE

Becoming a baal teshuvah involves both a significant change in life-style and values. As the name ("master of return") implies, it means finding the way back home. This simultaneous pursuit of both origins and transitions is a life-long process, but most baalei teshuvah begin consciously reorganizing their lives in late adolescence or early adulthood. Nevertheless, such a decision usually has its roots in much earlier experiences whose cumulative weight is the foundation for later change. Many of those earlier experiences are forgotten or their true relevance is not appreciated. Only seemingly disconnected fragments survive the selective and destructive processes of memory. Even so, an incomplete account is better than none at all....

Age five. It is summer time and impossible to go to bed while the sun still shines. Something might be missed! This will eventually grow into a desire to know the "whole" truth—nothing can be concealed.

Age twelve. I attend a typical Reform Sunday school. We visited local churches to observe our fellow Americans at prayer. There were, however, no visits to Conservative or Orthodox synagogues in the same town to observe how our fellow Jews prayed. We memorized twelve reasons why the Bible is the greatest book written by man (*sic*), but never once opened the text itself. We heard only Bible stories, summaries, digests, etc. Who knows what young, impressionable minds might see in the original! Our isolation from dangerous truths was thorough. Our texts had a short unit on Chassidism as an ignorant, superstitious sect in pre-war Europe; but they made no mention at all of the large, flourishing religious Chassidic communities in Brooklyn, less than an hour away.

Age thirteen. I had a typical Reform bar mitzvah. I was allowed to read unintelligible passages with flawless Hebrew pronunciation—and with zero comprehension—but was denied permission to sing the *haftorah* with its traditional melody. Supposed reason: variations in voice quality might put some other bar mitzvah to shame. I was allowed to have a great party, however, with no qualms that *that* might put some other bar mitzvah to shame. Summary: consumption, *yes*; cantillation, *no*.

Age fourteen. I attended a National Federation of Temple Youth summer conclave to swim, socialize, debate religious ideas and write "original" prayers.

Age sixteen. Three years after bar mitzvah and still "protected" from authentic Jewish sources, I attended a confirmation class meeting with our family's Reform rabbi. The inconsistencies were beginning to get to me. "Why should I pray in a synagogue? We Reform don't require a *minyan* or a fixed time or text for prayer. Why shouldn't I pray only when and how the spirit moves me?" "Oh," said the rabbi," that's because some day your parents will die and you will *have* to come to pray in the synagogue, and you won't know what to do." I remember being very unimpressed with the answer.

That was the year that the Director of Religious Education at our synagogue was sent on a year's tour of the U.S. to share the "success" of his educational methods with other Reform congregations. We students found that an incredible joke. Our goal, under his guidance, was to get out for good, and as soon as possible. That was success?

By age seventeen, even I had had enough. I left home for university as a confirmed atheist with no connection to anything Jewish. I majored in philosophy.

Age eighteen. Our Reform congregation sponsored student attendance at a "Jewish identity" summer camp in California. It was my first contact with passionate Zionism, and with Conservative and even semi-Orthodox Judaism. Revelation! There was much more to Judaism than I had ever dreamed, or had been allowed to dream. I resolved to make a thorough investigation.

Age eighteen. At university I majored in mathematical logic. I also took courses in Jewish subjects with anti-religious professors, which resulted in almost complete confusion! My fledgling attempts at minimal Jewish practice were made in almost total ignorance with no support system. There were less than ten observant students on the whole campus, and even these were less than encouraging. One Jewish student's response to my *kippa* was: "Who do you think you are, the Pope?"

My observance was initially rather erratic. On Shabbos morning I got up early to shower, cook (!) and eat breakfast. Then I walked to the chapel for services, being sure to tie my handkerchief around my wrist so as not to carry!

My introduction to the Bostoner Rebbe that year was another crucial revelation. Such warmth, intelligence, education, commitment and sensitivity in a supposedly "medieval" Jew! In a Chassid! In his Chassidic congregation full of college-educated mathematicians, physicists, sociologists, lawyers and doctors! Obviously a lot more had been hidden from me.

Age nineteen. There were more religious students on campus, and I was introduced to the *shiurim* (lectures) of Rav Yosef Be'er Soloveitchik, *zt"l*, yet another revelation! The Rav was a brilliant rabbi, a true master of Talmud with a doctorate in secular philosophy from the University of Berlin! My new weekend schedule became: Shabbos at the Bostoner Rebbe's followed by Rav Soloveichik's weekly public *shiur*.

My attempts to reconcile my secular, anti-religious college classes with the deeper insights of the Rebbe and the Rav resulted in more confusion. A typical gem from my professor of Biblical Hebrew concerned Gen. 24:63: "And Isaac went out to converse (pray) in the field...." It was now to be translated, he proudly pontificated, as "And Isaac went out to urinate in the field..." on the basis of newly discovered parallels with Ugaritic. This supposed "discovery" not only ignored Hebrew semantics and the fact that Isaac is explicitly described elsewhere as praying (Gen. 25:21), it also ignored the lack of a parallel for such a description anywhere in the Bible itself (the text supposedly under discussion). This was "serious" scholarship?

Ages twenty and twenty-one. Comparisons between my secular college classes and the teachings of the Rebbe and the Rav gradually began to yield clarity. By bringing the arguments of each side to the other for comment and rebuttal, I achieved a growing sense of the best-supported position.

I am, by nature, quite skeptical. My first three responses to any new idea are "No!" The fourth response is "Maybe", and then, perhaps, I can take it seriously. Judaism was no different. It had to survive all my best (and my professors' best) attempts to refute it. All sources of potential counterattacks were fair game: physics, cosmology, evolution, democratic social theories, epistemology and metaphysics, not to mention potential internal contradictions.

One minor example. To the traditional prayer "May He who makes peace in the Heavens, make peace for us and all Israel," I add "...and the whole world." After several months I casually ask the Rebbe if this is O.K. After all, Judaism does hope for universal peace, does it not?

"True, but such an addition is not appropriate," he answers. "Did you ever wonder what His making peace in the Heavens actually means? Are there wars among the angels? Rather, the angels know exactly who they are and what their purpose is; they suffer no identity crises. We hope that all people will eventually achieve that kind of consciousness; but the Jewish people must play the leadership role in bringing that result about. Now a leader must first believe in his cause. He must know for himself what he is to do and why. It is the peace of mind needed for leadership that we refer to in that prayer."

The Bostoner Rebbe soon became my personal spiritual mentor. More religious students came to campus, and we formed our own Organization of Religious Students. This led to clashes with the "establishment," in the guise of a Hillel rabbi determined to form his own brand of Reform/Conservative/semi-Orthodox hypocrisy on all and sundry. One example: We traditional students wanted services with a *mechitza*, a physical division between men and women congregants. We designed one in parts, on wheels, which could be used for our services and then, to avoid confrontation, be removed for the Hillel congregation's non-traditional services. The Hillel rabbi vetoed the idea on the grounds that any service held in the chapel must be one he would feel comfortable attending—even though he had no personal intention of ever attending it! The illogic of his position spoke volumes.

Age twenty-two. After receiving my B.A. in Philosophy and Mathematical Logic, I left for Jerusalem to learn full-time at Yeshivas Mercaz HaRav Kook (there were no baalei teshuvah yeshivas in those days). There I acquired fluency in Hebrew, serious exposure to Talmudic text and methodology, *Halachah*, *Tanach*, passionate Zionism, passionate anti-Zionism (in Mea Shearim) and A.J. Heschel (at Hebrew University). Myriad doubts were resolved, and I became committed to living in Israel, identified with Religious Zionism and Modern Orthodox Judaism.

I also gained new tools to deal with the sometimes well-meaning, but usually intellectually bankrupt, functionaries that had confused me in the past. A typical example was my meeting with the Director of Beit Hillel. At that time the Bnei Israel from India were protesting the decision of the Chief Rabbinate to require them to convert to Judaism. The Hillel director commented: "This is clear hypocrisy. We have authoritative responsa from five hundred years ago clearly stating that anyone who enters your community claiming to be Jewish should be accepted as such." He even showed me one such responsum. Impressed with his scholarship, I took his argument back to my yeshiva. Their reply: "Surely you now know more about the laws of conversion than that. That responsum was written when to be a Jew was only a liability. Being Jewish meant living in a ghetto, being excluded from various sources of livelihood, and constant persecution. Under those circumstances someone claiming to be Jewish was indeed believed. But today, as in the time of Shlomo HaMelech, being Jewish carries considerable benefits: automatic Israeli citizenship and financial aid in settling in Israel, both of which the Bnei Israel want. The responsum you were shown simply does not apply to such conditions."

Another time I heard A.J. Heschel assert: R. Akiva represents the mystic, the humanist, the political activist and the sympathetic philosopher; R. Ishmael represents the legalist: strict, elitist and removed from society. In contemporary terms, the Conservative movement represents R. Akiva and the Orthodox movement represents R. Ishmael; but traditional sources give R. Akiva superiority over R. Ishmael! The yeshiva's reply? Judaism does not decide serious matters of *halachah* on the basis of something as nebulous as someone's 2,000-year *post facto* perception of a sage's purported "philosophy." Furthermore, on several occasions R. Akiva's non-legal opinions are firmly rejected by the Sages of the Talmud (as in *Hagigah* 14a, *Sanhedrin* 67b, *Shmos Raba* 10:5 and so on). My feet began to touch solid intellectual ground. Things could be argued on the basis of objective facts.

Age twenty-two. My marriage to my life-partner marked the beginning of the most fulfilling life project one can have: creating a Torah-observant Jewish family. Back in America, I entered graduate school in philosophy.

Age twenty-six. I moved back to the States to teach philosophy at a well-known university. Our family became active members of the large and intense local religious community, although we still firmly saw ourselves as Modern Orthodox. In fact, by age thirty-one, I had already published an article in the Modern Orthodox journal *Tradition*.

From age thirty-three to thirty-six, I gradually become disillusioned with the Modern Orthodox orientation. I began to feel the virtual impossibility of maintaining dual religious and secular life-foci. I also became concerned by a perceived shallowness of Modern Orthodox scholarship in comparison with more traditional yeshiva sources. In particular, I discovered many mistakes in my own *Tradition* article. Why hadn't the editors caught my mistakes? This triggered a gradual evolution to a more Charedi-Chassidic position. Step-by-step, I began to adopt the Bostoner Rebbe's customs, eventually making a complete transition to the life of a Bostoner Chassid.

It has been an interesting life and an interesting process, one full of growth. Teshuva is the greatest creative challenge a person will ever face: the challenge of recreating oneself. A person's whole past—talents, training, experience, successes and failures—provides the materials from which his new identity will be forged. He does not turn his back on his past, but organizes it to fulfill its potential in a new way. It is a denial of Providence to regard any of his "unplanned" prior life as a loss. Everything which happened to him was planned so that he could fulfill his unique human potential and make his unique contribution (see Luzzatto's *Derech Hashem*, Part II, Chapter 3). Later, he will see how his seemingly pointless past gave him the tools for his religious future.

One important benefit of becoming religious later in life, through a conscious mature decision, is a heightened sensitivity to those aspects of Torah life which tend to become rote for others. Often this sensitivity generates insights from which all can benefit. A father once told me that he was nervous about speaking in public to deliver a *dvar Torah* for the *bris* of his third son. But then he began to wonder: why didn't speaking in front of Hashem Himself, cause him the same concern? He deduced that his prayer should be improved.

In my own case, working in *kiruv* (outreach) makes everything that I had previously learned relevant. It helps me communicate more effectively with people who are educated and talented, but who also want to be sure that Jewish society will understand and appreciate them. Even if one cannot see it at first, teshuvah is not so much a totally new beginning, as a redirected continuation leading to a new, higher goal.

⟡⟡

THE LIGHT THROUGH
THE WINDOW

In the early 1970s, as I transitioned from college to real life, my two-year relationship with a graduate student from Venezuela, culminated in a marriage proposal. My rather assimilated father's words still resounded in my ears: "I forbid you to marry him. You don't understand. You can't live as a Jew in Lake Maricaibo, Venezuela." Heartbroken and confused, I graduated college, ended my relationship, and moved to Boston to join the news staff of a local television station. I was twenty-one years old, totally assimilated, and only vaguely aware of my Jewish heritage.

The following spring, I was on a weekend assignment for the newsroom. I showed up on the doorstep of the New England Chassidic Center with a camera crew, ready to film the traditional baking of matzah for Passover. Curious and eager to bring back a good story, I stuck out my hand to introduce myself to the Center's leader, the Bostoner Rebbe. As I stood before him, in my jeans, boots, leather jacket and cap, his gracious response to my smile and attempted handshake was to throw his hands up in the air and tell me "My word is as good as my handshake!" With that we both smiled, and I knew I had just met someone who would have a profound impact on my life.

I set up the camera crew, looked around, framed the shots and, upon my departure, thanked the Rebbe for his kindness and promised to return the next day as a "civilian"—modestly dressed, and without nail polish and long nails. Instead, I would be a member of the Rebbe's community, participating in baking matzah. I came back the very next day as promised. And although it felt like entering another world, I knew—in the very core of my soul—that these people, these fellow Jews, were very much a part of every fiber of my being. Slowly, I began to untangle the threads of my own young life. My arrival at the New England Chassidic Center was clearly no accident.

Over time, I started to attend services, to spend Shabbos with various members of the Rebbe's community, to learn more about Judaism and to live a Jewish life. It was not an easy path for someone so assimilated. I struggled to balance observing Shabbos and keeping kosher with conducting my social and professional life in an appropriate way.

Neither my parents nor my older brothers were very supportive. In fact, they were concerned that I had fallen into the hands of some sort of cult. It was a challenge to earn my family's respect for my spiritual journey. I also met with prejudice from other Jews, including those from the *frum* community. Those who have been religious all their lives are often suspicious of baalei teshuvah, regarding them unjustifiably, as weak, lost or unstable. It was, and still is, a lonely journey.

Through it all, the Rebbe was always there, ready to help and guide, constantly respectful and non-judgmental. It was his voice that I heard above all others. Within a few years, I became *shomer Shabbos* and enjoyed the friendship and wisdom of people whom I still count among my dearest friends.

In the late '70s I returned to Connecticut, where I met and married my first husband, a Dane who had converted to Orthodox Judaism. We lived an Orthodox Jewish life, but ultimately our differences led to divorce. It was a terrible ordeal. My husband did not want us to divorce and made it extremely difficult for me to obtain a *get* (divorce certificate). It was a harrowing few years until the Bostoner Rebbe, in cooperation with rabbis in both Connecticut and New York, finally seized an opportunity to obtain a *get*. To this day, I remember that moment when the scribe in New York handed me the razor-slashed document he held in his knarled hands. "This *get*," he said delicately, quietly, but knowingly, "is so good, it would stand up in Israel." Little did I know what Hashem had in store for me, and how relevant that would be!

With my first marriage behind me, and my future before me, I returned to Boston to work and to reestablish my connection with the Rebbe's community. Along with me came the precious leaded glass panes of a stained glass window that had once adorned my grandmother's synagogue in Yonkers, New York. The building, which had housed Congregation Ohev Zedek for generations, had been recently destroyed by urban renewal. The window was my grandmother's lifetime achievement, honoring the generations of her family who had prayed within, a symbol of her great love for her community and Yiddishkeit. A few years after her death, just before the wrecking ball cut through the air, destroying the brick walls of the synagogue, efforts were finally made to save the window. All but abandoned by the congregation, the window was taken out, piece by piece, and it became my duty to find a new home for it. My father, disheartened by the indifference of the congregation and saddened by the death of his mother, never knew the fate of this window until years later...; it was still to have a major impact upon our family.

Upon my arrival in Boston, I contacted the Bostoner Rebbe and arranged a visit. I understood that he was building a synagogue in Har Nof, a suburb of Jerusalem. With me, I brought a white bed sheet and the leaded glass panes of the window. Spreading the sheet on the floor of his synagogue, I gently laid the glass down to form the magnificent seven-foot round window. I asked the Rebbe to accept the window as a gift for his new synagogue in Israel. The Rebbe graciously agreed and the window was redesigned (to fit) and prominently installed in the Eastern wall of his Har Nof synagogue. I was so grateful I could honor my grandmother's memory, and my father's great love and respect for her, in this special way.

A few days before Rosh Hashanah, the Rebbe called me from Israel with the news that the window had been installed. I was overcome with emotion. I called my father to tell him what I had done, and that this year grandmother's spirit would be a light in Israel. His unsettling silence on the other end of the phone was followed by my mother's voice: "What did you just say to your father?" she asked. My father, such a powerful presence in my life, had been rendered totally speechless by this gesture. My heart was full. In an instant I knew how fully I had honored my father by resurrecting the meaning and memory of my grandmother's life. Later, pondering pictures of the newly installed window, I wondered if I would ever have the opportunity to travel to Israel and see it in person. Yet it was there, in Har Nof, in the shadow of that window, that I was to be married a few years later.

Meanwhile, Boston was a welcome return to a vibrant Jewish community, the Rebbe, and my work as a high-powered marketing executive in the financial services industry. I continued to learn and, four years later, I was introduced by friends to the very special man who has since become my husband. I was delighted to learn that the Rebbe knew their family well and that he was pleased with the match. The third leg of my spiritual journey was about to begin.

As an international sales director for a high-tech firm, my husband had spent a great amount of time in Israel, Italy and Turkey. Over the years, he had made many friends abroad. Our plan was to be married by the Bostoner Rebbe when he returned to the States from Israel that fall, and to honeymoon in Israel and Italy. When we contacted the Rebbe in Israel to discuss our marriage plans, he suggested that we move the date up and come to Israel before Passover to be married in Har Nof. We agreed.

And so, on the ninth of Nissan, 5752, my husband and I were married in Har Nof, not far from my grandmother's window. As we stood under the *chuppah* (wedding canopy), surrounded by friends, overlooking the beautiful hills of Jerusalem, all the planets of the universe seemed in alignment. I was now part of the millennia of Jewish life, melded with the holy land. That evening at my wedding reception, the Rebbe reminded me that it was sort of an anniversary for us as well. We, too, had started a special journey together just before Passover, nearly twenty years earlier.

My husband and I returned to Connecticut and, several years ago, we adopted a beautiful little girl we named Sarah. When she was seven months old, we brought Sarah to the *mikvah* in Boston for the immersion. The Rebbe's son, Rabbi Naftali Horowitz, and two other respected members of the Rebbe's community participated, and we celebrated the event at the Rebbe's home in Brookline. We named her Shulamit Shifra, after my father's mother and my oldest brother, a"h. Now, each Shabbos, Sarah drinks from the beautiful little silver *Kiddush* cup the Rebbe gave her, and, every year, just before Passover, the Rebbe and I wish each other happy anniversaries.

My life has been blessed with great joy and burdened with deep sorrow. The Rebbe has always been there for me: my brother's passing; during my divorce; my second marriage; my attempts at fertility treatment and adoption; my father's surgery, terminal illness and passing. I've often thought of the Rebbe's selflessness, how he has helped thousands of people over the years, listening to our questions, hearing our anguish, celebrating our joys—he experiences them all.

How do you thank someone for giving his life to others? Perhaps via the resonance of his teaching and guidance passed from generation to generation. *Sheyich'ye L'orech Yomim Tovim, Amen!*

∽◌∾

THE ROAD TO SPIRITUALITY

Certain scenes stand out in our childhood memories, as "snapshots" or prescient summaries of our later life. My early childhood was no exception. In particular, at some time during their life, people have to choose whether to be basically "good" or "bad." I made my decision to be good in 1959, when I was five years old.

It was playtime and, standing next to our backyard seesaw, my older brother told me that Nazis were "worse than policemen." His explanation was necessary because, although I feared and hated policemen, it was the first time I had heard about the Holocaust. We were about to play "Jews and Nazis," a new version of Cowboys and Indians; and I had to choose whether to identify with the victims or with their oppressors. Mind you, most Jewish children in our neighborhood invariably preferred to play Nazis! This seems psychologically explicable. In a dysfunctional family, children also tend to identify with the abusive parent, rather than the victim. In both cases, the "bad guy" appears to be the strong one, and the "good guy" appears to be a weakling. Besides, why suffer?

In real life, as the family whipping boy (or girl), I took my siblings' corporal punishments, but I was still perceived as the strong one emotionally. Should I have behaved badly, since I was being "punished" in any case? The Holocaust game helped me define, for myself, the terms "bad" versus "good." To my five-year-old mind, "bad" (Nazi) meant, "Do whatever you want regardless of the consequences to other people." Being "good" (Jew) meant, "Do the right thing even if it hurts or makes you look like the loser."

Why, then, would anyone choose to be "good"? I got hit in any case, so why not have some fun and be bad along the way? But I had to live with myself. If I behaved well, at least I would be able to go to sleep at night with a clear conscience. That became my five-year-old creed.

Mother called my brother and me inside for dinner. Playtime was over, but I was a changed person, although no one else knew it. Every moral choice I have made since has been predicated upon that fateful decision. And, yes, I do sleep well at night.

If one childhood snapshot was morality, another was curiosity. I'm inquisitive by nature. I am always searching for truth, and I have to find things out, for myself. For me, this meant using the scientific method: are the results reproducible? If not, they are worthless. If so, they approach *The Truth*. I was also a bit of troublemaker, and soon learned—and repeatedly tested—the limits in which I was being raised. My mother called me a *kochleffel*, a stirring spoon. I didn't really do anything bad, but I liked to have lots of "activity" going on around me.

At four years old, I followed my mother around the house, not to help her, but to store information away in my memory banks for later retrieval and application (fourteen years later). I played with my older brother's train set while he was at school, because, after all, why should I and the train set be left behind at home! At eight years old I looked into a miniature microscope charm that my father gave my mother for her charm bracelet. No one else had ever done so, and I discovered a "secret message," a tiny inscription saying, "I love you," surrounded by little hearts arrayed in a heart-shaped pattern.

When I was ten, my oldest sister caught a wild rabbit and caged it in our garage. I let our cat into the garage and opened up the cage to see what sound rabbits make. The rabbit made it's first—and last—sound, something like "meep." As a high school senior I dissected animals in Biology II and at home, in order to see how they were "made." My mother permitted each jarred and formaldehyded specimen into our basement in turn, except for the fetal pig. It looked too much like a human fetus, and had to be dissected in the garage—where the rabbit had been devoured years before. I ended up using the same dissection kit years later in medical school.

A third snapshot involved the tension between religion and hypocrisy. Conservative Judaism, in which I was raised, began to seem persistently and increasingly inconsistent. If it was really O.K. for the congregants to drive to the synagogue on Shabbos, why couldn't the rabbi do the same? Why did we ride to synagogue on Shabbos, but walk on the High Holidays? Why did we furtively park two blocks away and then walk to an Orthodox Bar Mitzvah, if it is was really O.K. to be Conservative? And if dual standards *were* an option, why did my friend's classmates at his Conservative Hebrew high school laugh at him when he wore his yarmulke even *outside* of Bible class?

Why did my father's Conservative colleagues laugh at me when—at eighteen years old and newly observant—I stepped into the hallway to avoid *davening* at a *mechitza*-less weekday *minyan*? And, if truth was a virtue, why did my teacher at the Conservative afternoon school write me a negative reference as a "punishment" for my piety, instead of refusing to write one and telling me straight out what bothered him? And what about the Division Head at my Conservative summer camp, who was "too busy" to write me a reference altogether? The questions kept piling up.

No problem. I was leaving the "movement" anyway. Why? You can chalk it up to a kind of spiritual biology. True-bred animals reproduce replicates, whereas hybrid animals, as genetic mosaics, don't breed true. In my views, Conservative Jews, like hybrids, don't breed true, generation after generation. Most of their children either become Orthodox or leave institutional Judaism altogether. I, myself, am a Conservative "dropout." In medicine, a conservative mastectomy preserves the underlying pectoralis muscle; a radical mastectomy excises it. Conservative Judaism sustains a forty percent loss each generation because of intermarriage and a low rate of reproduction. Actually, I wouldn't call that conservative. I'd call that pretty "radical!"

[Twenty years later I confronted my afternoon schoolteacher. With a straight face, he baldly denied having written me a bad reference. I still occasionally see both the Division Head and the Educational Director of my former Conservative summer camp. They're my neighbors in Jerusalem. I know who they are, but they haven't quite succeeded in placing me. And my old, Shabbos-walking, "closet-Orthodox" Conservative Rabbi has finally come out of his closet and now *davens* in our local Orthodox shul in Jerusalem! I get to greet him all the time. His wife and my mother used to carpool together.]

My last "snapshot" shows me as a college freshman in 1971, about to meet the Bostoner Rebbe, R. Levy Yitzchak Horowitz, *Shlita*. I first went to the Rebbe's shul in Brookline, Massachusetts on Simchas Torah night. His shul was *the* place to go—notwithstanding a three-mile walk each way. Beth Pinchas was a nice place to visit; and the Rebbe and Rebbetzin were nice people. They seemed so natural and unassuming that one just took them for granted. What I did appreciate about the Rebbe, almost from the start, was his caring about me as an individual—unqualified, unconditional love. No one had to tell me that my necklines were too low, nor my hemlines too high. I was finished with the, "How can we change Judaism to fit the modern age?" of Conservative Judaism; but I wasn't yet ready for changing myself to fit *halachic* (*Haredi*) Judaism. I was still trying to learn how to live a Hashem-centered, Torah-observant life. I had only begun to truly appreciate the Rebbe, when I left Boston for medical school.

A good friend once said, "The only thing more amazing than how many people love the Rebbe is how many people he loves!" Indeed, the Rebbe makes his greatest impact one-on-one. This is reflected in the many unique—often surprising—unpublished decisions the Rebbe has made for individual Chassidim, on a highly individual basis, over the years (which should *not* be taken as generally permissible positions). For example, when my medical school status was in jeopardy, he allowed me to walk the eight miles to and from my parent's house to the hospital on Pesach, but urged me to try to do the generally forbidden *melachos* necessary for my training with a *shinui* (change), if possible. He also told me to choose the residency that would make me a better doctor, even if it was not *shomer Shabbos*, unless I'd be so unhappy with a Shabbos-violating program that I wouldn't be able to learn anything anyway! Finally, he told me that through the proper observance of the laws between Man and G-d, and Man and Man, I could make my medical practice and indeed, my entire life, a *kiddush Hashem*.

The Rebbe took into account where I was holding spiritually and always sought to affect qualitative, though subtle, improvements.

Conversely, he once told an over-eager baal teshuvah, who prematurely started wearing Chassidic garb, to put away the externals and to work on his internals first! Even today, at the Bostoner shuls in Brookline, Massachusetts, and Har Nof, Jerusalem, people come "as they are." No one is turned away, and the Rebbe tries to accept each Jew "as is." Change is effected through love, by example, and, yes, with a healthy helping of humor.

One Friday evening, after services in Brookline, the Rebbe was greeting each congregant one at a time, as they headed down to the *Kiddush* in the basement. One hippie-type, male college student asked the Rebbe, quite innocently, "How are you feeling, 'Rebs'?" The Rebbe answered him equally casually, and not at all caustically, "Frankly, I'm pooped!"

The Rebbe often described his early failure as a diamond polisher. I once told the Rebbe that, on the contrary, he had been a highly successful diamond polisher. He had taken college students "in the rough," cut away their rough edges and polished them until their true value showed through.

On Becoming
a Ba'al Teshuvah

The process of becoming a baal teshuvah is a deeply personal one, and I doubt that the external history of my quest would be particularly useful to anyone who is not really me. Instead, I will try to concentrate on the internal aspects of my journey and—setting aside worrisome doubts about the accuracy of memory—distill broader perspectives that might be helpful for those that follow.

What led me home? I can, with effort, discern three main themes in my own Jewish development: the desire not to miss, the rejection of arbitrary limits to investigation, and the desire for an integrated world-view. A few words about each will have to suffice.

Not to Miss. The world is a many-splendored place! What an endless variety of opportunities to experience and understand. I have always wanted to know and experience something about every thing (and even to master a few). I attended the National Music Camp in Interlochen, Michigan, have performed many times as a classical flutist, learned to sail in camp, wrestled in high school and ran track in college. I hiked as a boy scout, and I had my own campus radio program as a college freshman.

To me, a denial that something is real is suspicious. It reduces the world's potency and, therefore, must be backed up by a solid proof. My Reform Jewish "education" had left me without any significant Jewish connection; but when it became apparent that much had been carefully *concealed* from me, I was not content to merely take the newfound information and apply it. I wanted to make sure that even more information wasn't still missing!

Hiding the truth was a conscious, widespread policy of the Reform. In Pittsburgh a woman, introduced as Orthodox, spoke to a class of Reform students. One asked about the "tassels" attached to the corners of Jewish garments. The supposedly Orthodox woman responded: "They are called *tzitzit*. The Torah says to put them on the corners of garments; but no one does that any more!"

Many attended the same Jewish "consciousness-raising" camp that I did; but their consciousness rarely raised them beyond visiting Israel, marrying Jewish and occasionally attending a (non-Orthodox) synagogue. This, of course, is a great deal considering their start from total non-identification. In my case, however, Hashem led me on to mind-stretching university courses, invaluable connections with the Bostoner Rebbe and Rav J.B. Soloveitchik, and a year at the Mercaz HaRav Kook Yeshiva in Israel. Later, the same curiosity led me to explore Chassidic life, organization and yeshiva scholarship, which carried me beyond Modern Orthodoxy into the Charedi world.

Limitations on Investigation. In every area of study I found assumptions which were regarded as unquestionable within that area. I found such limitations artificial. Why are *these* chosen as the axioms of mathematics? Why is *this* the scientific method of investigation? Why are *these* the tools of linguistic analysis? Such unanalyzed assumptions were intolerable. I was therefore attracted to philosophy, which at least tries to examine every element of investigation without prior arbitrary assumptions. On the same grounds, I found the blithe dismissal of religion—which was fashionable in chic, liberal university circles at the time—highly suspicious. This suspicion was reinforced when I found that their superficial reasons for rejection were easily rebutted by Torah giants such as the Bostoner Rebbe and Rav Yosef Baer Soloveitchik. Even the laymen in the Rebbe's congregation, who often had advanced degrees in mathematics, physics, medicine and law, could easily answer these supposedly conclusive "refutations." The Association of Orthodox Jewish Scientists made it even clearer that cosmology, evolution, etc. do not pose insuperable problems for religion. One need not rely upon arbitrary limits and unjustified assumptions. Those who think that religion necessarily requires an irrational leap of faith are simply applying non-Jewish ideas to Judaism.

Integrated World-View. The philosopher seeks to understand everything, to create a comprehensive structure within which everything fits, in which each thing's uniqueness is registered and its relationship to everything else is portrayed. The Torah is such a structure. It is truly comprehensive. Theory and practice, fact and value, the physical and the spiritual, the individual and society, intellectual and emotional approaches, past, present and future—nothing is excluded. Essence and relationships are both governed by the same fundamental insight: how each thing serves the Creator's purpose for His creation. Once there are adequate reasons for accepting such a world-view as true, it is hard to ignore on philosophical grounds.

These same considerations eventually led me to Chassidic philosophy and practice. Chassidic thinkers, especially R. Tzadok Hacohen, take up the entirety of the tradition at once and show the integrated organization of the whole. Typically, they start with several puzzling passages in the Talmud, *Tanach*, Midrash, legal codes and commentators. They then cite a Kabalistic idea to provide a deep theoretical explanation which renders those passages understandable. In the process they reveal a deeper unity in the tradition as a whole. What could be more exciting to a philosopher? Chassidic practice has the same effect upon action. A human being encompasses intellect, emotions, attitudes, motivations and actions. All have to be woven into an integrated whole. The appropriate expression of love and caring, thinking and feeling, giving and receiving must be delineated. Rav Soloveitchick once wisely said that *homo sapiens* must become *homo deliberans*. Under the guidance of the Bostoner Rebbe I found all this within Chassidism.

Once the inner mechanisms of teshuvah were in place, the rest followed—despite occasional detours—fairly automatically. I will spare you the personal details, which may not apply to others, and concentrate on six strategies which would seem widely applicable to others starting out on this road. I found them indispensable to navigating the hills, sharp curves, speed traps and occasional falling rocks, when I set out on my way.

Gradualism. Small steps taken consistently build solid spiritual growth. Rapid changes can cause a loss of psychological integration which can threaten the whole process. Different parts of the personality change more or less easily in different people. The enthusiasm of a new form of life often leads to identifying with those parts which change easiest, while leaving the other parts behind. Eventually, the gap becomes too large to tolerate and the person feels "out of sync" with himself. Even good, honest people can exceed their spiritual speed limit. I remember one fellow who came into a summer program completely non-religious and by September was already wearing a black hat and suit. In January, already disoriented, he told me, "I *daven* every morning, but half the time I don't know if I am not just talking to myself." Another fellow learned in a yeshiva in Jerusalem with a ponytail. When he cut if off after six months, the staff was concerned—this was too soon for him.

Two types of gradualism are necessary: setting priorities among the different areas in which progress needs to be made and subdividing each area into small, manageable steps. There is no hypocrisy in not making a full transition in one "great leap forward," despite Chairman Mao's catchy phrase. This is true for at least two reasons: First, it is not possible! There are simply too many areas which need attention to address them all simultaneously, so priorities must be set. This is true even for those with a prior religious background. Certain matters must be left for a later occasion. Second, a hypocrite says he believes in something, but does not make a sincere effort to achieve it. Setting strategic priorities is not insincere, particularly if an immediate full transition is impossible!

Allies and Environment. A person is always affected by his social environment. Even if one could withstand a negative environment without deterioration, he would be needlessly using spiritual energy to prevent that deterioration. In a more positive environment, he would have achieved even greater spiritual growth! Therefore it makes sense to seek out as positive an environment as possible, consistent with one's other commitments (family, education, profession, etc.). Continuous Jewish study—including good study partners, classes and access to a Torah authority able to answer both practical and theoretical questions—is especially important. Regular contact with religious families (Shabbos, holidays, etc.) is crucial for gaining religious life-experience.

The need for a supportive environment is not a confession of weakness. Remember everyone else is being supported in their *non-religious* lifestyle by their *non-religious* environment! It also does not mean a retreat into a self-imposed ghetto (although that's not always bad—consider Joseph's plan to settle the Jews in Goshen to weaken the influence of the majority Egyptian culture). Work and community affairs will dictate more than enough interaction with the non-Jewish world. But, for that very reason, a spiritually positive home environment is necessary to freely express and reinforce one's own identity.

Avoiding Conflict. It is not the neophyte's job to change the world, nor even his own family and friends. His job is to manage his own adjustment in as integrated fashion as possible. That should be hard enough! His relationships with others should be respectful, and he can always hope for equal respect in return. He is not responsible to correct everyone's misinformation and prejudices. He should not be afraid to confess ignorance: his few months or years of study, starting from virtually nothing, need not qualify him as an expert. On the contrary, since he has seen considerably more than the vast majority of his contemporaries, he need not feel that his commitment or cause is undermined by his personal inability to answer specific questions. He need not know everything; but he should know where to turn to for authentic answers.

Indeed, the best strategy for handling antagonistic challenges is to provide the challenger with the name and telephone number of an expert who can best respond to his criticism. The next time the same person challenges, the beginner can politely inquire, "Did you speak to so-and-so about the last question you asked?"

Another, admittedly difficult strategy is silence, especially in public. If someone says, "Everyone knows that religion is medieval, superstitious nonsense!" How should one respond? Well, how would one respond if someone said, "Everyone knows that the Democrats (or Republicans) are incompetent liars!" The best response is dignified silence. Bystanders will then note that the speaker is obviously behaving offensively and immaturely, whereas any response will lead to a two-sided controversy, in which both sides will be presumed to be equal.

One should also be aware of how one's word choices and approach can inadvertently generate needless conflict. For example, a beginner should not speak of *choosing* a way of life. That sounds too final; and, besides, one cannot be truly sure that one's new enthusiasm will last. Instead, one should speak of *exploring* a lifestyle. That is both more accurate and a good way to defuse potential conflict. It is very difficult to attack a young person for merely exploring. Similarly, a beginner should not present what he has found as "The Truth." That description can mask a desire for control or manipulation, for it implies that everyone else must conform and soon. It thus invites a charge of fanaticism. Rather one should put his enthusiasm in personal terms: it is meaningful, challenging and inspiring to *me*.

Finally, *vis-à-vis* parents, one should stress how the values they taught helped bring him to his present position. Often differences over Shabbos or *kashrus* wrongly overshadow the essential ultimate commitments that they share. His parents taught him the value of honesty, justice, love, sensitivity, scholarship, courage, independence and sincerity. These are a basis for attraction to a way of life that has represented and realized these values for millennia.

Substance and Style. Many baalei teshuvah become convinced that the Torah is true and try to observe as much of Jewish law as they can, but become bewildered by the wide variety of styles of traditional observance. In addition to broad differences of philosophy and priorities (Modern Orthodox, Yeshivish, Chassidic, etc.) there are endless geographic variations. Having no personal tradition to fall back on, they must decide for themselves, without waiting for a comprehensive investigation of all options. In fact, at the beginning of his exploration, the baal teshuvah is usually introduced only to a very small sample of the alternatives—often only one. Still, one cannot postpone having a single, consistent organizing style to his observance (I've seen the mixed up results of trying to form one's own supposed "synthesis.") The solution is to adopt a style temporarily, and to explore alternatives as time and circumstances allow. In the meantime, one remains committed and open to change. This requires clear communication with others who depend upon him, such as his spouse, children, etc., since any subsequent changes will affect them as well.

That's what I can remember about the practicalities of the journey; but perhaps I can say a bit more about the emotional aspects of becoming religious. For me, the dominant feeling was one of incredible excitement and exhilaration. The challenge was truly great, taxing all my talents and resources, but there was never any serious doubt about my (or anyone's) ability to succeed. My teachers made it clear that dedicated effort would surely be rewarded. I was never worried that my life would come apart and that I would be left with useless fragments. Of course, there were uncertainties; but they added to the excitement of the challenge. There were also mistakes and local failures; but I took them as a normal part of any long, complex effort to achieve something as precious as it is difficult. The continuous opening of new vistas of understanding and experience—both of the world and myself—was, and remains, endlessly fascinating. Although not everything was done as well as it could have been, nothing was pointless; every mistake eventually contributed improvement. In brief, I experienced no serious regrets. The most painful part of the transition was reaching mutual respect and understanding with my parents, *a"h*—which may have happened quicker if I had met my wife sooner. But even there, the end was a solid success.

Along the way, I made many precious friendships some of which continue to the present day. Breaking into serious Jewish scholarship was, for an extended period, a source of some frustration. My prior secular training, while superb, was not ideal preparation for Talmud.

Still, had I not crossed that threshold, there would have been a painful lack of self-respect in my Jewish identity. Today, all aspects of Jewish study provide endless challenge, insight and the satisfaction of being a competent member of the international brotherhood of *lomdei Torah*. Most of all, I feel endless gratitude to Hashem and to those who served as His agents to make all this possible. It's been a long road home...but a road well worth traveling.

You've Got It Made:
Peers, Presidents And
Professionals

"Futility of futilities," says Koheles, "Futility of futilities, all is futile. What does a man gain by his labor which he does under the sun?"

Koheles 1:2-3

The School of R. Yannai said: He has no [profit for his worldly labors here] under the sun, But [for his Divine service whose origin lies] before the sun, he does.

Shabbos 30b

People have all kinds of dreams: wealth, prestige, power. All distractions, says Koheles, are a meaningless empty substitute for the real prize, a life of *kedushah* (holiness), which is hidden behind the gaudy facade of this world. These are strong words, but from the mouth of a great king and sage—someone who had already "been there, done that"—they carry great weight indeed. In every generation there are those who awaken to these great truths, for whom it is no longer enough to dream of the sheaves of this physical world; and like Joseph, they begin to dream of the stars beyond.

REAL ROYALTY

Much has been written about becoming a baal teshuvah, whether through sudden illumination, turbulent struggle or gradual growth. My story is not about that, although I went through many of the usual stages as well, but rather about what comes next. In particular, one is inevitably left with the "problem" of one's past. Should baalei teshuvah continue to cut away at their personal past, finally leaving them as disembodied as a Cheshire cat, with no face and only a smile? Should they feel guilt, shame or self-derision at their origins or lack of background? Should they feel themselves "second class" Jews when interacting with the *frum-from-birth* community?

Everyone knows the "politically correct" answer to these questions, but can a baal teshuvah really feel what he should, rather than what he does? The results can be more than just psychologically stressful; they can be tragic. How many *gerim* (converts) and baalei teshuvah have ended up in inappropriate marriages, not only because the established Jewish community didn't feel that they deserved better, but because they *themselves* didn't feel that they deserved better?

This may not describe my own case exactly. I was born into a mixed family, with a nominally Jewish mother. My first marriage, while not always happy, ended largely for other reasons. Still, what to do with the past—that long tail that forever follows one around— is a perennial problem. In my case, I paradoxically reintegrated large parts of my past and my personality, while pursuing my *non*-Jewish roots. That led to my learning more about my relationship to two lines of kings, one physical and one spiritual.

I became a baal teshuvah in the States and a Chassid in Israel. On my way back to the States from Israel, after my divorce, I stopped over in England. I knew that my mother's family had come from a certain Jewish neighborhood in London; but, when I went to visit, huge office buildings already covered the entire zone. Few signs of the area's Jewish past remained. Instead, I noticed the stately British College of Arms down the street. My mother's father (but not her mother) had been non-Jewish, and was reportedly of noble descent. Remembering the family coat-of-arms over the mantel back home, I decided, with nothing better to do, to trace my genealogy. Of course, dressed in my long black Chassidic frock-coat and round black hat, not to mention a beard and *peyos*, I seemed rather incongruous in this inner sanctum of the British peerage.

Just one look and the receptionist immediately pointed me away from the genealogical offices, towards the souvenir and postcard rack near the front entrance. Several of the other workers and tourists snickered quietly at my unusual garb. When I noticed a sign offering "Genealogical Services for a Fee," I went back up to the desk and asked about it. When I said that my grandmother's maiden name was Hastings and I mentioned several other related facts, her expression changed from amusement to frank puzzlement. She introduced me to the appropriate clerk. I set out my questions, paid the fee and left for the States. Later, Herbert Cheshire, the Lord of Arms, wrote me back and said that he had found three possible connections for my family; and he asked for additional information. I sent him a copy of my grandfather's coat-of-arms, along with 50 pages of notes from my great-uncle in Connecticut.

Eventually they proved our descent, through my great-grandfather, James Goodwin Hastings, to Henry, the Third Earl of Huntingdon, and to his great-grandfather, the Lord Chamberlain Sir William Hastings (who was beheaded by King Richard III, as related in Shakespeare's famous play of that name). Sir Williams' great-grandfather, John Hastings, was a claimant to one-third of the throne of Scotland. One of John Hastings' other great-grandsons married the daughter of King Edward III.

The Hastings family was originally part of a group of Danish Vikings who came to England during the reign of King Alfred the Great, and who adopted the name of their leader Haestingus. The Hastings were close to the monarchy from Norman times, serving as stewards to William the Conqueror, who invaded England from France, in 1066.

Several Hastings families had to flee to Connecticut, in the New World, in the 1600s, because their noble lineage posed a threat to Queen Elizabeth I. Many others became Puritans. Their descendant, my maternal grandfather, Elliot Hastings, was also rather a rebel. He completed high school in three years, Yale University in three years, and then headed West to California to prospect for uranium. He did not find his fortune; but he did find and marry my Jewish grandmother—although neither of them, unfortunately, had much interest in their respective heritages.

My discovery of my roots alternated with my trips, three times a year, to visit my children in Israel. I longed to return to Israel, and I struggled to save every penny I could to both support them and to move back myself. On each trip I stopped in London for more genealogical research. I finally got into the family's old synagogue, now rarely used, but information on my Jewish family was scarce. In contrast, the College of Arms now allowed me free access to their dusty old rooms full of ancient handwritten manuscripts.

Every time the reaction was the same. People snickered at my "odd" appearance, until Herbert Cheshire, now the King of Arms, would whisper a few words to them, and they suddenly blushed and treated me with respect. Cheshire even invited me to Windsor Palace to attend the annual presentation of Knights of the Royal Order of the Garter. He assured me that my garb would be no problem, since they were already used to noble American eccentrics! In the end, my schedule didn't allow me to attend, but the irony remained. In the States, during my early baal teshuvah days, I had often been laughed at when I had claimed to be Jewish; and now, in England, I was often laughed at when I had claimed to be British nobility. And it had taken a lot of digging to uncover my past and rightful place, at least on one side (alas, I never did find a distinguished rabbi on my mother's side).

On a visit to Windsor Castle, where one of my great uncles lies buried next to King Edward IV (their mothers were sisters), I found many rooms roped off and photography forbidden. I simply mentioned my lineage and Herbert Cheshire to a curator, who said, "Why didn't you say so!" and personally escorted me to all the closed rooms connected with the family, encouraging me to take pictures along the way. On another trip, the same thing happened at Ashy de la Douche, which had been partially blown up by Cromwell. My papers admitted me on Sunday, when the castle is closed, and I roamed at will through that once splendid manor, free to reflect for hours on the end of all temporal majesty.

I left through the cemetery where I sat, for some time, by the grave of my great-great-grandfather Henry Hastings. My musings were interrupted by a pack of English schoolboys giggling at my Chassidic clothing and jeering me as a "filthy, money-hungry Jew." They started to throw sticks and rocks, showing to good effect the kind of courtesy they had learned at their school, founded by "the beneficial and good graces of the Noble Lord Hastings."

My stay in America had also been less than smooth. Two weeks sufficed to make me realize that I couldn't stay in my parents' home. I spent one month with one brother, in New Jersey, and then moved on to another brother in Vermont. Realizing that an Orthodox Jewish environment and community was a must, I then found a job in Boston. There I met the Bostoner Rebbe, who taught me a whole new way to regard my past—how to not reject and be embarrassed by it, but how to emphasize and up-lift the positive. My interest in my background was one way to better relate to those parts of my past, a way to know myself better, and to serve Hashem with all aspects of my personality.

My first wife was always acutely embarrassed by my past, my non-Jewish father and my only vaguely Jewish mother. She passed that embarrassment on to me, and I always had to suppress that part of myself—what I was and what I had been. My second wife was far more understanding; she even had a longstanding interest in Elizabethan England (how's that for *hashgacha*?). The two once met and my first wife complained about our children knowing the "dark secrets" of my past. "Did he ever tell you about his *yichus* to the Queen of England?" she said sarcastically. My current wife answered, "Why, of course. I know and the Bostoner Rebbe knows, and *he* can accept it," and then looked straight at her. She just looked away, said "Oh," and fell silent.

I became very attached to the Bostoner Rebbe and began attending his *tish*. I would help his *gabbai* whenever I could, and gladly lent him a hand in the kitchen. One day the *gabbai* was out and the Rebbe asked me to pour wine for him. My ancestor had poured wine for King William the Conqueror; but I was extremely nervous. I had visited Buckingham Palace and Windsor Castle as an "insider," but now, on this Shabbos with the Rebbe, I felt in the presence of true royalty. After the meal ended, and all the guests had left, I went over to the Rebbe and told him how fitting it was that a physical descendant of the Kings of England should now be *zocheh* to serve a spiritual descendant of the holy Baal Shem Tov.

GETTING WHERE?

I was in a panic. My *sheitel* was not looking as I hoped, and my frustrated hands were just making things look worse. Comb in hand, I tried to do what only experienced *sheitelmachers* achieve, in a few minutes. I wanted to look nice; it was my priority at that moment. I tend to live like that now. Small priorities, one at a time. The phone rang. The ringing swirled me into more of a fluster. "Let it go on the answering machine," I said through the closed door. "It might be important," my husband replied. "It's for you." "Please tell them I will call back on Sunday, we are running late as it is."

"I think you should come to the phone," he insisted. Zooming out of the bathroom with a look on my face that mirrored my sadness at not having much *mazel* with the *sheitel*, I swooped up the phone.

"It is the Rebbe," the voice said. "How are you? The Rebbetzin enjoyed your visit yesterday." It was the Bostoner Rebbe. How wonderful to hear his voice again. It had been a long time. I put down the comb and changed my focus.

I had sat with his Rebbetzin for an hour the day before. She was feeling a bit low. Medical issues were restricting her life now and it was not a comfortable situation. When I arrived she was not in a talking mood, so I suggested my telling her our current family news. She agreed, and I helped settle her into the recliner chair. Smiles and laughter followed. It was like old times. We used to spend a lot of time together before I got married. A few years had passed now and there was a lot to tell her. Usually, I updated things with monthly letters and photographs mailed to their home in Boston. When they came to Jerusalem, for their annual six-month stay, I would see her a few times a week.

During my family update, I had told her that I was writing a book about my journey to *Yiddishkeit*. That was why the Rebbe was calling me now, although he had called me only a few times since we had met seven years ago. Since it was only a few hours before Shabbos, he was right in thinking that I would be home. "I am also putting together a book," he explained. "It's a book of baalei teshuvah stories and I want to include yours." I excitedly responded that I would be thrilled to be part of the Rebbe's book.

For a week I thought about what I wanted to write. I had so much to say, and the Rebbe wanted just a "contribution." Where should I begin? While I was with my Rebbetzin and teacher, the wife of the Torah leader Rabbi Chaim Pinchas Scheinberg, I decided on the beginning of my piece. I shared my idea with her and she agreed it would be an excellent start.

My story is a long one with lots of ups and downs and winding paths. However, my journey has also had a myriad of powerful, enriching moments that may interest you. I have been through hundreds of miraculous and transforming experiences, and although it is impossible to tell them all here, these few stories will reveal to you why I feel we should all be trying to "come home"— to get closer to Hashem, ourselves and others through a Torah way of life. A material life without spirituality is a sad, empty and meaningless space in which to live. My experiences have taught me the harsh reality: the difference between mere physical existence and emotional survival, and living a holistic enriching life centered around Torah connection, growth and challenge.

• • •

My conversation with the Bostoner Rebbe immediately transported me back to my own first, incredibly powerful, life-changing jolt. Picture a confident, self-assured, attractive, high profile young executive. I had been working since I was eighteen in the glamorous world of fashion public relations and was influenced and inspired by an elite crowd of international fashion designers and media. New York, Paris, Florence and Milan were familiar cities for me, as I flew here and there, enjoying my hectic and stylish life. Not a graduate of any university or ivy-league school, I felt that I was achieving all this on my own merit, so you can imagine the state of my ego.

When I was around twenty-two years old, I was "head-hunted" to work alongside a team setting up a dynamic new public relations company within a very successful, high-profile advertising agency. I thought my life had really taken off. My ego and my inflated self-image became out of all proportion to reality. I had got caught up in the "London High," riding the ego wave, showing the world you can make it when you are young! I freely chose to be part of the scene, at the expense of good relations with my parents and old friends, who were emotionally abandoned in the euphoria. Yes, I was delighted to share with them my successes and press cuttings about my latest business wins, however, a part of me got lost in the process.

A year into my new job, they offered me a lot more money and the privilege of a company car. I was bringing in a lot of good clients and making a lot of noise in the trade and public media. Money and perks, however, were not my key motivators. I am not really sure what really kept driving me on and on. I never made time to think about it, or anything else too deep for that matter. I had more superficial things on my agenda. Boyfriends were also a thing of the past. I did not have time for personal commitments and all the emotional energy required to maintain even a half-decent relationship. Life was one big party—work hard by day, play hard by night. In fact, at times, night and day merged into one, the pace was so fast. I was in love with my life and myself.

Then one hot breezy day, the bubble started to burst. I left work a bit later than usual. The sun was setting and the night sky was aglow with an orangey red radiance. I took the roof down on my Volkswagon convertible and put on a music tape. Before I drove off, I caught a glimpse of myself in the car mirror and was pleased with the way I looked. My long hair fell onto the shoulder pads of my new designer suit; and my skin was still tanned from a recent trip to Europe. I felt good.

At the next red light, I had to stop facing a tavern where a lot of young people were taking in the pleasant evening air over a glass of wine. My boss, sitting at a sidewalk table with a large group of colleagues, proudly looked over and shouted, "Hey, look at you. You are really on the way up. You are really getting there." He winked at me. I stared at him for a long moment, and then I took the curve in a hurry, catapulted into deep thought.

Getting there? Where? The words flew around in my head like an unwanted fly. They buzzed so loudly that I had to stop the car, a little way down the road, to catch my breath. I felt almost like I was going to faint from the feelings that were overwhelming me. In a lightning flash, I realized that the fast life I was living was an empty and shameful existence. It was going *nowhere*. I began to sob uncontrollably. What was I doing? Was that my life, and the way people saw me? A true picture of my essence and potential as a person? I made a call and cancelled my evening arrangements.

Sitting alone in front of a blank pad at home, I started to write down all the things on my mind. If you took away all my external looks—my position, my work, my car, my bank account, my clothes and possessions, my filofax diary with my business and social telephone numbers and calendar listings—what would be left?

"Nothing!" I scribbled in large letters across the page. It was an awful picture. Did I have a meaningful relationship with anyone? Was I capable of helping someone before myself? Was I working on improving my character or trying to become a more giving and compassionate person? Did I have a capacity to think beyond what suit to buy or which contract to sign?

Since childhood, particularly in my fast-track secular world, I had been conditioned to believe that ownership, professional standing and financial means gave a person security, respect and purpose in life. There may be some truth to that for a lot of people; but I now felt that I could not support the rest of my life on those principles. There had to be something else out there for me. I was determined to find someone or something that could lead me beyond my old perspective and seemingly empty "truth."

The next stage of my life was a challenging and rewarding, if chaotic, period. Looking back, I think that Hashem was really watching over me and could see that I was sincerely trying to find Him. I could easily have been lost on the winding path I had been traveling. After abandoning all my previous held ideals, I began taking calculated risks. It took a lot of courage and guts, but I started to create my own pattern of self-discovery. I sold my apartment and rented a room with an elderly lady. This was unheard of in our family, which enjoyed all the luxuries that accompany a successful father. I did find renting with a stranger unfamiliar territory; but I needed a change now and renting a room for a while fit in well.

I was desperate for a lighter load in life with less commitment to London. Maybe the challenge ahead included finding a different place in the world to live. Just because a person is born into a certain family, place or lifestyle, does it have to be that way forever? Maybe those circumstances do not bring out the best in that person. I felt now that this was definitely the case for me.

To maintain a semi-secure financial position, I took on short-term temporary jobs as a personal assistant to department directors in interesting television and publishing companies. It was great for me. In between my contracts, which lasted between six weeks to six months, I started to travel around the world, searching for answers to all the questions that were now surfacing in my heart and mind. The Far East became a favorite destination, since materialism was not the center of the universe there. Wherever I went there, I encountered lightness and an unusual spiritual energy. Through reading and meeting new people there, I found new religions and new understandings of life and spirituality. Tibetan Buddhism, in particular, seemed to encompass many of the new values that I felt were vital for my emerging soul: truth, compassion and wisdom.

My life in London also became much more pleasant. By weaving Tibetan Buddhism into my life, I started thinking that, maybe, I could now spiritually survive life in London. However, still driven to travel, I first wanted to experience more of Buddhism in its original context. I decided to go to India first, planning to continue on to Tibet. In India I had many vivid spiritual, emotional and physical experiences, which turned me in a new direction. They are too numerous to mention; but, when I returned from my six-week visit, I started speaking to Hashem.

In His Kindness, Hashem heard my desperate cry for guidance and helped me. He led me a few months later onto the path of Judaism. I really believe that prayer saved me from getting lost in a place where so many other Jewish souls are still suspended. (Tibetan Buddhism is an honorable and sensitive religion; but I have come to understand that, for me, it is really just an offshoot of the real thing, the Jewish way of life.)

Rabbi Tatz, a mentor and inspiring Torah scholar, tells a story in his book, *Anatomy of a Search*, about a boy who was traveling the world looking for truth, just like I was. He ended up in an *ashram* in India, a place where people go to focus on spirituality. He became so enthralled and excited that he asked to meet the head monk, to express his thanks. (You can tell he was a Jewish boy. Only a *Yid* has such a true instinctive capacity for *hakoras hatov*, gratitude.) He was finally granted an audience and, after pouring out his thanks, the head monk suggested that he go study Torah in Jerusalem. The boy was astounded. "I, too, am Jewish," the head monk said, "and I think you should go and learn about your own religion."

I also nearly ended up in an *ashram*. It was on my agenda after Tibet. I may not have been so fortunate as to have such a giving and amenable head-monk to guide me back to Jerusalem. Hashem had a different plan for me. In India, I came face-to-face with a baby Hindu girl, a few hours old, lying on a dirty carpet, among the poor street people. As I looked into her dark brown eyes, with tears running from my own, I realized that my fate was not sealed like hers, and maybe it was time to find out if there was something for me in my own religion.

When I got back from that trip, I started to ask Hashem for help and, very soon after, he "arranged" for me to meet a new girlfriend who took me to the Jewish Learning Exchange, a street away from my rented flat. With little more than a few pounds in my purse, with no real job to my name, and a feeling that I did not know what the next day would bring, I entered the new world that was my own heritage. It was an inherited gift from the generations of my grandparents, a world that brought me eventually to Jerusalem, to my husband, to my two little boys, to being a *frum* woman, *sheitel* and all.

To my amazement and joy, the integration was smooth and a relief. Now my whole being is in a place that is fulfilled and satisfied. Life is more meaningful and special, more balanced and harmonious. It is shared the world over with other *frum Yidden* who value the same Torah outlook and vision that my husband and I try to live by each day.

All I can say, at this point of my journey, is that Hashem is miraculous. Hashem hears all our prayers. Give Hashem a chance. Give Judaism a chance. If you really want to "come home," Hashem will watch over you and will guide you all the way.

JUST TAKE THE FIRST STEP.
THE FIRST JEWISH PRESIDENT

When I was in junior high school I had it all figured out: I was going to be the first Jewish President of the United States! My parents already had interested me in becoming a lawyer, and my father was involved in local partisan politics. Like father, like son. I started a local Democrat Youth Organization. I was managing more than a hundred 12-18 year olds by the age of thirteen. By the time I was sixteen, I was the county leader and, by age eighteen, I was the statewide leader of the Young Democrats. I was on my way up the ladder of success. I was already in a prestigious university, would graduate with honors, go to an Ivy League Law school and, with my Democratic Party connections, I would get a great job clerking for a Supreme Court judge. From there I would run for Congress and then, after 3 or 4 terms, would run for the Senate. The rest would be history. I would be the first Jewish President!

Then Sirhan Sirhan put a bullet through the head of Robert Kennedy and my dreams were shattered. I was no longer the leader of the Young Democrats. I was a young man with my big ambitions buried along with Robert Kennedy. To put it mildly, I was very disturbed. I did not want to climb up any ladder to this form of "success." I routinely finished my second year of college in the late 1960s and joined my share of anti-war demonstrations and smoke-filled parties. My parents were very concerned—where had all my idealism gone?

I was groomed from an early age to try to be the best. I was the first grandson of a second generation Jewish family—a typical story. My great grandparents were all *shomer Shabbos* when they came to American in the early 1900s; but slowly the effects of America wore them down. After a few years, only my maternal great grandmother remained *shomer Shabbos*. Her name was Sara Gittel and, although a boy, I was, more or less, named after her. (Gittel, "good" in Yiddish, became Tuvia, "good" in Hebrew).

My great grandparents sent my grandparents to public schools and observed Shabbos, unless they had to work, and kept kosher, at least in the house. When my grandparents were married, they didn't observe Shabbos and, if *treif* meat was cheaper, they bought it. Still, they spoke Yiddish and knew how to *daven*. My parents grew up in Brooklyn. And what was Judaism to them? A few Yiddish words their parents spoke, when they did not want the kids to understand what they were talking about.

And what was Judaism to me, the third generation? I still remember the whole extended family getting together in Brooklyn for Rosh Hashanah and my mother's father saying *Kiddush* on the first night. Walking to shul and playing with the *tzitzit* of my grandfathers and great uncles helped me pass the time in the gigantic Orthodox shul where they were big contributors. I did not know what was going on, but I liked the songs and reading from the Torah scroll. It was different and somehow other-worldly. My favorite song was *Ain Kelokenu*, because it was at the end. The annual ordeal was finally over!

Then we would relax in the bar, drinking beer or *schnapps* and watching the baseball game before returning for *Mussaf* and *shofar* blowing. In the afternoon the extended family would gather together around one long table—the food was great—*lukshen* (noodles), gefilte fish, *cholent* and *kugel*. Just coming for the food was worth it. On Yom Kippur we did not eat, not even me; but the feast after the fast was unbelievable, with all my great aunts and uncles, aunts, parents and cousins—a real shebang.

What did I get from my parents? A lot of love and affection and attention to help me make it big. They gave me lots of trips throughout the States, summer camps, fun home activities—a really great childhood. I also had one sister and two brothers to fight and laugh with. We were all brought up to be individuals. In short, we were a typical, dysfunctional, Anglo-Jewish family, with no centering family activity—just running to do and do and do something, as long as it did not hurt anyone else. Christmas trees and presents, sometimes Chanukah. Purim, what was that? Pesach, we could hardly wait till we finished with the Maxwell House Haggada so we could eat. Shavous—uh? I went to Hebrew school, but I would have rather been playing baseball. I was brought up to succeed, and I was succeeding until that fateful day.

Hashem works in very mysterious ways. In the beginning of the summer of 1969, our local Reform rabbi contacted my parents to enroll me in a UJA Youth Leadership tour of Europe and Israel. I didn't have anything else to do and thought it might be fun. So off I went on a whirlwind tour to Paris, Vienna, Munich and Bucharest for three weeks, followed by five action-packed weeks touring the length and breadth of Israel. We visited ORT schools in Paris, met with the heads of Jewish welfare organizations in Vienna, saw movies of the concentration camps and visited Dachau, Mathausen and Auschwitz. We visited with the Chief Rabbi of Romania and met with kids our age who wanted desperately to live in Israel.

In Israel we received the red-carpet treatment, spoiled Americans having the time of our lives. It was exciting! We met with kibbutzniks, socialists, Oriental Jews from Yemen, Arab sheiks with seven wives and 87 children, and even spent a Shabbos in Jerusalem. We met an Air Force general in a war room, went swimming in the Red Sea and water-skied on the Sea of Galilee. We stayed up all night in Safed, went to every museum in Tel Aviv and ate at the best restaurants and met the most prominent politicians (there were a lot of them!). We had roundtable discussions on Israel and its future. We were being groomed to be the future leaders of Jewry in America. Our future job was to stay in the States and rise in importance so that we would make it, become rich and give money to support the Zionist state.

Only a funny thing happened. I got an unbelievable desire to live, not in the States, but in Israel. During the summer, I was accepted to the University of Manchester and went back home to get my clothes and see my parents. I didn't want to live in the States anymore, and I was glad to finish up my college years in England, away from all the anti-war demonstrations and drug culture. During my first week in England, we were asked to write an essay on why we wanted to study abroad. My essay was modestly entitled, "Searching for the Meaning of Life."

I started to take courses in philosophy and psychology. In the back of my mind I always knew that I would live in Israel, but did not connect that with anything in the diaspora. During my final year of college I decided to read and do everything that I had always wanted to do. So I stopped going to all classes except for a psychology class called Mysticism. The professor was a gentile English psychiatrist, married to a Jewess. He was a really interesting person, who had scientifically mapped out changes in heartbeats during different stages of meditation. I loved to meditate with him, and we would talk outside of class about India, meditation and Karl Jung. I read all of Jung's books that year. I was developing emotionally and trying to make sense of life.

One day he asked me, "You're Jewish, right? Why don't you study about your own mystical tradition? It's called *Kabbalah*." That made sense. I was Jewish and, true to Jung, believed in the "collective unconscious." So, the next time I was in London, I visited a Jewish bookstore and got a book entitled, *The Ten Luminations*. I really connected with this book, written by one of the students of Rebbe Ashlag who had translated the Zohar into Hebrew. Then I got the Soncino translation of the Zohar and I really felt that I understood every single word. I must have read those five volumes at least ten times, over and over again. Everything made sense to me now. I was Jewish, the place to live was Israel, and the book to study was the Zohar.

One night, which I later realized was the *seder* night, I had a mystical experience. I was in my bed when I "saw" that my body had levitated off the bed. Really! I turned to view the lightbulb in a stand next to the bed and it expanded, keeping its shape, and then exploded into a thousand pieces kept together by visible, hot melted air. At the same instant a tremendous burst of luminous energy swept through my body, from my feet up through the crown of my head and the lightbulb returned to its original state. I woke up and, for the next few days, everything was buzzing. Trees were occupying the place of themselves, people had auras surrounding them, water was velvet, air was visible. I had so much energy flowing through me that, the next day, I started doing really detailed abstract colored ink drawings. They were quite good. I saw things differently. It was time to speak with a rabbi, not with a gentile psychiatrist. I went to the local Hillel House, but the rabbi wasn't in; and the place did not look that enlightened to me anyway. There was nice music playing in the background, though, and for the next few years I always hummed the tune I heard there.

I finished college and went back to the States. My upscale parents really did not know what to do with me. I spent all my time drawing and painting, reading Jewish books on mysticism and having these very highfaluting conversations with them about Israel, mysticism and the Garden of Eden. The most tangible thing in my life was my artwork. My mother was an artist and interior decorator, and I was encouraged to take photography courses, something practical. I commuted for a few months to Manhattan and completed a basic darkroom photography course, while reading the Zohar on the commuter train. City life was not the place for a real artist, so I moved into a little cozy house on a stream in the town of Woodstock, where my family spent the summers. I continued to paint and to look for a rabbi. I went to Crown Heights a few times, but it wasn't my cup of tea (as they say in England). I loved Woodstock and teamed up with a Sufi guru and meditated for hours in the forest, but I knew that my place was with a rabbi, not a guru.

One day I went to an exhibit of Mexican string paintings at the Whitney Museum of Art in Manhattan. There I saw a movie, in a sideroom, entitled "Spiritual Movements in America." Every single swami and guru was in this movie, and there was a token Jew, a rabbi with a guitar and hippie musicians. I never saw a rabbi like this, Shlomo Carlebach. I liked him. He was cool and he was with it and he understood the Zohar and these guys were the type I could connect with.

As I mentioned before, Hashem works in mysterious ways. Two days later, on a lamppost in Midtown, I saw a poster announcing Rabbi Shlomo Carlebach at the Energy Center that night at 8:30. I was there at 8:30 and the first song that Shlomo sang was the song I had heard at the Hillel House in Manchester, years ago. To say that

I became *frum* on the spot is, maybe, an overstatement, because Judaism is very complicated; but you could say that I had found my place. I became a "Shlomo follower." Wherever he was, I was. I wore a very colorful yarmulke (after all I was an artist), I practiced vegetarianism (except for chicken on Shabbos), I loved music and I loved Shlomo. I loved Shabbos and I loved eating kosher food. Even my parents came once to a singing study session and they were happy that, at least, I had a kosher group to be with. Better that than the isolation and drugs of Woodstock.

Shlomo was *mamash* great. He was also always very late and always took a long time to get across a point. About the same time I met Shlomo, I also met another rabbi, Meyer Fund. He was a very concise and very deep, American-style Orthodox rabbi; and I started attending his classes regularly on Sunday mornings in the Brooklyn Young Israel shul. We also began studying the tractate *Chagiga* in the Jewish section of the New York City Public Library until we were asked to leave for making too much noise. So we moved to Touro College and started studying *Tanya* and *Nefesh HaChaim* at the same time. A great uncle sent me his old pair of *tefillin*, and I started putting them on everyday. I started relearning Hebrew and *davening* three times a day.

My *Zohar* sat on the bookshelf collecting dust, while the *Siddur* and Talmud were now being used. I was listening to Shlomo's music all the time and still looking for my ultimate place in the Jewish world. My sister was then living with her *goyish* boyfriend in Brookline, right across the street from the New England Chassidic Center. So I visited Boston several times for Shabbos to see my sister. I *davened* and ate with the Bostoner Rebbe, and always immensely enjoyed the Rebbe's warm environment—very American, very *frum* and very stimulating. To this day I have a special relationship with the Rebbe, and the Rebbe has always been there responding to those special questions that only a Rebbe can answer. But Boston was not my ultimate soul-connection. I was searching for something more outwardly other-worldly, something not connected to sequential time. I was looking for meditation and song and timelessness together. Williamsburg was not for me. Flatbush was not for me. I loved the *febregens*, but Crown Heights was not for me.

I had moved out of Woodstock for Manhattan, and was still painting and photographing to make some money. I even had a big show in a 57th Street gallery. I got a sales job in a photography lab to pay for the prints in the exhibition which was covered by several magazines. Hashem indeed works in mysterious ways. My new boss came up to me on the first week of my work, on a Thursday, and told me that his father-in-law could not go with him to Israel on a high-level fundraising mission Sunday night. Would I like to go with him on a cheap ticket to Israel? So I went to Boro Park Sunday morning and that evening I was on a plane to Israel.

I always knew that I would live in Israel; but it had been seven years since I had been there. So off I went, along with the address of Rabbi Nachum Bulman at Yeshiva Ohr Somayach. I was the only *shomer Shabbos* participant in the mission, so I had Shabbos off and went to Rabbi Bulman. He sized me up right away—art, music, Eastern meditation—and suggested that I meet the Amshinover Rebbe late Saturday night for *Seuda Shlishis* (usually an afternoon meal!). I took a taxi to Bayit Vegan and waited until 12:30 in the morning for the Rebbe to come.

This was the beginning of the end. When the Rebbe sang *Mizmor L'Dovid*, which took more than half an hour, I saw everything that I wanted to find wrapped into one. Here was art, music, meditation, concentration, this world and the next world in a pure Jewish form. I left in the middle of the night with the Rebbe's impression engraved onto my soul.

Two weeks later I was back for Purim in Boro Park. There I saw two young Chassidim dancing in the street in ecstasy. I asked them where they were going for their Purim *tish* and they said, "Amshinov."

What! Amshinov. I was just in Amshinov in Jerusalem. You mean there is also an Amshinov Rebbe in Boro Park? Yes! The first time I went to Amshinov in Boro Park was on Purim 1978. The Rebbe was a hidden *tzaddik* tied to the upper worlds. One of the Chassidim invited me to join their night kollel: not to learn *Kabbalah*, but *hilchos Shabbos* and grammar. I was thrilled. I worked during the day in Manhattan and studied at night. I was warmly invited by many families in the shul for Shabbos. I guess I was a novelty. Everything clicked. I changed my colorful *kippa* for a more conventional black one; and I started wearing proper dark suits with a white shirt and tie. I was really becoming committed.

Although my brothers and sister had thought that I had gone out of my mind before, they now thought that I had really gone off the deep end. It was a family decision that I should start seeing a "shrink" (psychiatrist). My parents kindly conveyed the message to me: "You have deep emotional problems that you could work out together with a trained psychoanalyst." I had no objections, just that they should pay the bill. I had a very close relationship with my parents, visited them every Sunday, and participated in all family functions that were not on Shabbos. I went to this doctor, a very warm person and the son of a Mennonite minister. He wanted to know all about my involvement in Torah. The third and final time I visited him, I was explaining the Jewish laws of family purity, which involve the menstrual cycle. He looked up from jotting in his notebook, with his reading glasses perched on his nose, and said, "I see that you have a phobia of blood. We will have to discuss this at a later time." That was my last appointment. There was no later time.

I returned to Jerusalem for Yom Kippur and Succos. Before Succos I delivered a message for a friend in Crown Heights to a couple in the Old City whose apartment overlooks the *Kosel*. They asked me if I was interested in going out to get married. I said yes, but not tomorrow, since I was going on a trip to the North. When I reached Meron, a few other *bochurim* asked if I wanted to go to Amukah.

I asked them what that was. It's a place; and when we got to the *kever* of Yonasan Ben Uziel there, they explained that this is where you *daven* for your soulmate. I guess I *davened*, because the next day I met my future wife. We met six times and our conversations were very deep, and we decided we wanted to create a Jewish home together. But first she wanted me to meet her rabbi, so we sat and he grilled me trying to find out if I was normal. After all, I was an artist, a Shlomo follower, a new follower of the Amshinover Rebbe, and I had never learned anywhere for any period of time. This had all the markings of an unstable personality.

But Hashem works in mysterious ways. The son-in-law of the Amshinover Rebbe of Boro Park was this rabbi's cousin and he happened to be in Israel at that time. After speaking with him on the phone, the rabbi came out of the kitchen and said, "*Mazel Tov.*" I returned to the States to work and my *kallah* followed three months later. That summer we were married, with the band playing the Shlomo *niggun* that I had first heard in Manchester, *Od Yeshamah*. We immediately returned to Jerusalem, where we live and are raising our daughters to be *yiros Shamayim*.

I guess I will leave it up to someone else to become the first Jewish President of the United States.

THE LONG, LONG JOURNEY

I grew up in a town in the American Southwest. Our family was nominally Reform, but there was never any religion at home, not even on the holidays. I went to Sunday School and rode to Shabbos School and had a bar mitzvah, but what we learned I don't know. My mother never lit Shabbos candles, and we always worked, and never fasted, on Yom Kippur. We never even heard about most holidays. In short, I came from a very secular background.

In 1974, during the last year of my medical residency at the University of Colorado, my medical school advisor mentioned that he was going to India for a year. He lived outside of Boulder, in the spectacular foothills of the Rocky Mountains, on land homesteaded by his grandfather. His large spread had access to thousands of other totally pristine acres, all very beautiful and peaceful. I asked him, "What are you going to do with your house while you are gone?" He answered, "I'm going to try and rent it out." So I began thinking to myself: "Maybe I'll sell my house in Denver and move up to his house for my last year." There happened to be a nearby bus that traveled to the medical center and back every day. And that's what I did.

While there, I used to go hiking with a postgraduate anthropology student, who often mentioned the world's greatest composer was Beethoven. So I went to a store across from the medical center and bought Beethoven's Sixth Symphony, conducted by George Tsell. One day, I came home early, sat next to a window that faced all the beautiful mountains and trees, and listened to this amazing music. I was taken to another universe; I had never experienced anything like that before. It was a very spiritual thing. This was the first thing that started me on my journey.

The second thing was a chance *Denver Post* article on Thomas Moore's book, *Utopia*, written in 1555 and placed in America. Many years before I had bought a copy on sale (for 10 cents!), but I had never read it. Inspired by the article, I found the book, read it, and my mind exploded. Then I began reading about other utopian communities in America. In fact, I lived only 60 miles or so from Greeley, Colorado, established by Horace Greeley ("Go West young man...") as a utopian community. I read about the Mennonites who fled religious persecution in the Old World and about the kibbutzim in Israel.

I also had leisure time, for the first time in my life, and began hiking alone, for several hours or even days. Arizona had been totally different than the pine-covered canyon where I now lived. I used to sit for hours watching the canyon's clouds and the changing water, streams and snow. I saw birds and snakes fighting for survival and a newborn deer. I went skiing and saw lichen on the rocks—orange and brown and green—every color you could imagine. I became much more aware of what was around me. Ann Dillard's book, *A Pilgrim at Tinker Creek*, also made me more aware of my surroundings, and I became much more animated than ever before.

Another book from that era had short, capsule biographies of many famous Jews. I saw a Nobel Prize winner here, another Nobel Prize winner there, and a discoverer of this or that. Then I started to realize how many famous violinists, pianists and so on were Jewish. I suddenly became very aware of who was and who wasn't Jewish. I remember walking around the hospital seeing all these people who I never realized were Jewish. I even remember asking people, "Are you Jewish?" Some said yes; some, no. I did my residency with a *frum yid* from Denver who went to Y.U. Years later, he came to visit me in Jerusalem. He looked at me, with my beard and *kapote*, and said, "I can't believe it! All those nights together, and I never knew *you* were Jewish."

When I finished my residency, I traveled with a friend to the Orient, before starting my medical career at the Center for Disease Control (CDC). We flew to Japan for two months and then Okinawa, Taiwan and Hong Kong. There we took a ferry to visit a beautiful monastery on Lan Tow Island. Just as we got off the ferry, I met a Harvard-educated, Chinese fellow who was a student of Buckminster Fuller, the inventor of the geodesic dome. We spent quite a time speaking and, when I got to Singapore, I started reading Fuller's books, all very interesting. Fuller graduated Annapolis in 1912, convinced that you had to know how to fix things, improvise and innovate. He said that he could go into any scientific discipline and, within a couple of minutes, get down to the cutting-edge of knowledge in that particular field. I was intrigued because, intellectually, that's now what I wanted to do too. I actually heard Fuller speak in Vancouver, Canada, a year later, and was still very impressed.

Another book I found in Singapore was *The Sleepwalkers* by Arthur Koester, a self-hating Hungarian Jew. I had previously read his book *The Thirteenth Tribe*, which claimed that Ashkenazi Jews had no connection with *Eretz Yisroel*, but rather were converts from the Kuzari, people who lived between the Black Sea and the Caspian Sea. In *The Sleepwalkers*, he claims that the Greeks were close to understanding the mechanics of our solar system, before Plato and Aristotle took a different path and the older insights got lost. They were revived by Copernicus in the 14th century and buttressed by the Danish Astronomer Tyco Brahe.

I read his book on the beautiful island of Bali, the only non-Islamic area in Indonesia. It is the archetypal paradise island; but, when I finished *The Sleepwalkers*, I said to my friend: "You know where I really want to be? In the New York City Public Library! There is a whole world out there, but all I've known for the last eight years is medicine. I want to be an astrophysicist or a mathematician or a nuclear physicist and take one of those disciplines beyond its limits, to where it becomes philosophical, even theological."

We continued on to Australia and New Zealand; but my relationship with my friend had begun to change. I went back to start my CDC job in Olympia, Washington, where my love of Beethoven and the piano led me to take piano lessons. (That eventually helped me woo my wife; I played the first movement of the "Moonlight Sonata" for her one day!)

I spent all my spare time at the piano, sometimes practicing 5-6 hours a day, and reading. I read about 120 books—history, philosophy, Aldous Huxley, things that gave me an overview of what was going on in the world. I did read a little paperback on the world's great religions, but it didn't make much of an impression.

There was a symphony orchestra in Olympia, and I asked my piano teacher to arrange a visit to a rehearsal. During the intermission, a young teenager came over and asked, "Who are you?" She was rather eclectic, wearing a Star of David, a cross, a crescent and a peace sign. I became friends with her and her whole family. The mother was a nurse (and perhaps Jewish) and the father worked for the Fish and Game Department. All three daughters were musically inclined. They had also adopted an Afro-American young lady and a Jewish fellow who had learned in a yeshiva but was now working for the telephone company. My friend took me to a Rosh Hashanah service and later to a *seder*, but I didn't really *chap* (grasp) what was going on. The family also had a huge telescope and they showed me Jupiter and three of its moons. Having read *The Sleepwalkers*, that sight blew me away. Jupiter was so many millions of miles away, and here I was seeing it with my own eyes. It was unbelievable.

My tour of duty at the CDC finally came to an end. The two people who were supposed to be teaching me were at odds on everything, and I hadn't really gotten much out of it. I didn't really know what I wanted to do. Perhaps I wanted to be an astrophysicist, but that was rather impractical. Realistically, I had to do something in medicine.

Lo and behold, one day, I saw an advertisement in the *New England Journal of Medicine* that said, "Are you interested in studying the pathogenesis prevention and treatment of Lassa Fever, Marburg Virus, Ebola Virus...anthrax?" all really weird, tough, infectious diseases. It was an offer from the U.S. Army Medical Research Institute in Frederick, Maryland, the Army's old biological warfare center. Since I had gotten out of the Marines as a "conscientious objector" back in 1972, at the height of the Vietnam War, my Army records were not exactly the best; so I figured they would never take me.

The next week, I didn't see that ad. The following week, I did. I took another look and said, "Boy, that is really what I would like to do!" Still, my old commanding officer had said, "This man is inimical to the welfare of U.S. military troops." I called anyway and they said, "Come at our expense and we'll discuss things." I walked around the institute and I told them frankly, "Look, I don't know the first thing about research, but I do know that what you do is what I am interested in." They said "Fine. We will teach you everything you need to know." So I signed up. They wanted me to start in July; but I said, "Wait, I'll start in November, because I have to go to Jerusalem for Rosh Hashanah and Yom Kippur." I don't know where that came from. It just popped out of my mouth. They said "O.K., make it in November."

I had no real idea of what Rosh Hashanah was...I just knew I had to be there. So I left Olympia for Jerusalem and my life got back into gear. I drove down to Southern California through the back roads. When I visited some friends from my internship years they said, "Wow. You are on fire." I, *mamash*, could feel it. I had so much enthusiasm. My "conscientious objector" lawyer explained that "enthusiasm" comes from the Greek *en* (within), *theo* (god) and "ism." It is the state of god being within a person—how we should be all the time. My friends had to shield themselves from the radiation of my intense inner energy. I could feel it myself.

In Southern Arizona I visited my parents. My sister had become friends with the rabbi of the local Young Israel synagogue and she took me there on Shabbos (we drove of course). That was the first time I had ever been inside the shul, only one block away from two of the houses I had lived in. They *davened*, but I didn't know an *aleph* from a *beis*. I didn't know anything. At *Kiddush* I met a *frum* fellow from MIT, who was doing post-doctorate work on planetary movement. He said, "Oh, you are going to Israel? Come to my house tomorrow night and we'll chat." So I went over and we started to talk and, at one point, he showed me his *tefillin*. Now I was almost 36 years old and I'd never even heard of them. I thought he was crazy. I almost fell off the bed. He put on those box-like things. Why? He didn't really explain it, but he said that this is what Jews do every day.

I continued across country in my Saab, mostly on back roads. I saw all sorts of wonderful sights until I came to Kentucky. You can't travel on back roads in Kentucky, because they only go a mile or so before they stop. Then it was all highway until New York, and the plane to Europe.

I had been to Europe several times before. I hiked the French Alps for a few days and then headed to Prague to stay with a Catholic friend, Vladimir Dubin, whom I had met on a previous trip. I told him, "You know, Vladimir, I heard that the oldest continuously used shul in Europe is here in Prague." He said, "Yeah. I'll take you down there on Saturday." Fine. We go down there on Shabbos, by tram, and I walk in. There were only about ten men; some young like myself. One was a *ger tzeddek* with a long beard; one was from *Eretz Yisroel*. Several of the old people looked like they had seen hard times. Part way through the *davening*, a white-haired man came over to me and said five words in English: "The Germans destroyed our lives."

Back in Colorado, in the middle 70s I had read about the Holocaust. I could hardly believe it, even 30 years after the end of the War. I checked out a whole bunch of library books on Jewish history and, one day, I backpacked with my little dog up into a little hollow carved out by rain on a small mountain, surrounded by forests, trees and hawks. I began reading and then I started to cry. I suddenly realized that the Holocaust was the same thing that had happened to the *yiddin*, wherever they had lived, for centuries. It was new only in its scientific expediency. So I cried. My cousin had married a man who escaped with half his family from a concentration camp in Czechoslovakia. So I knew about the Holocaust.

Later in the *davening*, the man came back and rolled up his sleeve to show me the number tattooed on his arm. At the end of *davening*, he came back and said another five words "I still believe in G-d." When he said that, something hit me. I don't know what's going on here! I've really got to find out what is going on in this world.

At *Kiddush*, I began talking to a fellow who had just returned from Israel. He told me, "If you're going, you have to take this special Sinai tour." So I took out my pen on Shabbos, and in the Maharal Shul, started writing down the info. Suddenly, a tall skinny old man came up to me and screamed, "It's Shabbos!" The pen went flying out of my hand. I didn't know you couldn't write on Shabbos. Who would have known that? I felt very bad.

In Greece, I revisited the island of Idra, near Athens, with a family staying at my *pensione*. We took a little boat to a part of the island where I had never been before. The family went off on their own, and I started walking down a wadi by myself. I stood there, in the middle of nowhere, all alone and, all of a sudden, the little bushes in that hot, barren mid-summer landscape seemed to move. It was the most unbelievable sight. All of a sudden I realized that I was so hot and thirsty that I might be having a heat stroke. I had nothing with me to eat or drink, and I didn't even know how to get back.

I turned around and saw, right there on the side of the wadi wall, a fig tree leaning over perpendicular to the ground. I had never eaten a fresh fig before. Zillions of ants were running out of the open ones; but I picked a closed one off and ate it. It was *mamash* delicious. In my own way, I gave real thanks, although I didn't know to whom, or anything like that; but I was very thankful that the tree was there. Later, on the island of Crete, I was reading Descartes when, all of a sudden, all of the things that had happened, and all the things that I had read, came together. I decided, "This world has to have been created. It just fits together too perfectly to have come through blind evolution. It doesn't make any other sense to me." My thought was not rigorously intellectual; it just seemed to pop into my mind.

In *Eretz Yisroel*, I first stayed in Tel Aviv with some relatives of my father, z"l, from Warsaw, Poland, who had immigrated in the middle 30s. They were nonreligious intelligentsia—philosophers and scientists. They advised me to take the train up to Jerusalem, but I missed the train and had to take the bus. At the Jerusalem bus station, there was a sign that said, "If you haven't been to a yeshiva, you haven't been to Israel." It was signed by Aish Hatorah. I looked at it, but it didn't click.

I went down to the Old City and the *Kosel*, and I wrote a little note, "Please save Israel...whatever," and put it into the Wall. Then, all of sudden a man, Meyer Schuster, came up to me and said "Hi! What's your name? Where are you from? Where are you holding?" I told him my story. "Very interesting," he said. "How would you like to meet a philosopher who is also a rabbi?" I said "Sure." So he took me to Reb Noach Weinberg, the Rosh Yeshiva of Aish Hatorah. I was probably Reb Meyer's easiest customer, because that was where I really wanted to be, even though I didn't know it at the time.

I spoke for a half-hour to Reb Noach. He told me a story about an angry, young American he had recently met. The fellow complained, "I've been all over the 'Holy Land,' but I didn't see any holiness." So Reb Noach asked, "Perhaps, but how many blobabows did you see?" The man asked, "What are blobabows?" but Reb Noach simply insisted, "How many did you see?" Confused, the fellow complained, "Well, if I don't know what they are, how can I tell you how many I saw?" "Hum," said Reb Noach, "And *kedushah*? Do you know what that is? If not, how do you know that you *didn't* see it?"

So Reb Noach sent me into the *beis medrash*. It was parshas *Ki Savo*, and I started learning from a linear English/Hebrew version of the *Chumash* with Rashi. That was the first time I had ever read *Sefer Devarim*, and *Ki Savo* talks all about the *tochacha*, Divine rebuke. I had just come from Czechoslovakia, with heavy exposure to the Holocaust; and, reading the *tochacha*, I realized "This is *emes*. This is the truth. Hashem warned us. If you don't follow My ways and My Torah, this is what is going to happen to you!" I was, *mamash*, in shock.

I could be in Jerusalem for only another three weeks, before starting my Army job in Maryland. I had also already paid $100 for my Sinai tour, which ended Erev Rosh Hashanah in Eilat, too late to get back to Jerusalem. I mentioned this to Meyer Schuster and he grabbed me by the collar, lifted me off the ground, and said, "You can't! You have to be here for Rosh Hashanah!" So I stayed. And I stayed on for Yom Kippur as well.

One Friday afternoon I visited a friend from my hometown, who worked for the *Jerusalem Post*. She and her roommate were watching TV and I picked up a little book about *Adam Harishon* when, all of a sudden, I remembered, "I can't be here! Shabbos is coming soon. I have to be back at the yeshiva." I had been away touring for a few days; and, when I reached Aish Hatorah, it was *gone*! I knew it was the right place. I remembered the doors, the walls, everything...but the yeshiva itself was gone! Inside there was one broken desk, but no *sefarim*, nothing. I couldn't imagine what happened. What was illusion, and what was reality? It was here just two days ago—now it was gone. I finally found out that they had moved.

Once safely back at yeshiva, I was the last one to go to bed at night, and the first one up in the morning. I was on fire. I was reading the *Chumash*, something I had never read before, and I could hardly believe what I was reading. My last week in the Old City, I walked around as if I were a prince of Israel from thousands of years ago. I was just imbibing the atmosphere—incredible!

About three o'clock one morning, I woke up and decided to go down to the *Kosel*. Two old men left just as I arrived. I stood in front of the *Kosel*, all by myself. All of a sudden, my ears started to ring as if I was in some kind of magnetic field. All of sudden, all my misconnections seemed put back in their proper place, and I saw clearly, for the first time, what it meant to be Jewish. I realized that my whole life had been lived backwards. The 248 mitzvos *asei*, the things you should do, I didn't do any of them, unless by chance. The 365 *lo sa'asei*, the things you shouldn't do, I did them all, or would have. I stood there and cried and cried and cried, until my pants and socks and shoes were soaking wet. Eventually people started to come for *v'sikin minyan*, before dawn, and I left a different person.

I wanted to stay in *Eretz Yisroel* and learn, but I had to go back to America before Succos, as promised. So, in one hour, someone taught me a six-week course in how to *daven*. I bought a little pair of *tefillin*—I had already had *tzitzis* and a *kippa*—and that's how I went back to Fredrick, MD. On Friday night, before Shabbos this time, I drove into town and parked my car near a shul. I wore a Yemenite *kippa* and stood in the back with my *tzitzis* hanging out. After the service, the rabbi came up to me and said "*Shalom Aleichem!* Who are you?" I told him my name and added that "I am here to learn Torah and do *mitzvos*." He looked at me like I had just come from the moon. He was an old Telshe Yeshiva Yid who had been in this town for twenty-two years, waiting for somebody to say that.

He took me home for the Shabbos night meal. I could barely read Hebrew, and it took me about an hour just to say *Kiddush*. And that's how I became religious.

I heard a story, several years later, about how the first Lubavitcher Rebbe, the Ba'al HaTanya, had been jailed in Czarist Russia. His jailer, a devout Christian, once came to see him with a burning question. "If G-d knows everything, why did he ask Adam '*Ayeikah*'? Where are you? Didn't he know where Adam was?" The Ba'al HaTanya replied, "Tell me, Mr. Jailer, do you believe that the Bible was given to all people for all times?" "Yes. Yes I believe that with all my heart." "Then know that Hashem asks that of all men at all times. 'Where are you?' Not physically, but spiritually. Did you make My world a better place? Did you live according to My laws? What have you got to show for your years?" [And here the Ba'al HaTanya specified the jailer's exact age.]

I now know myself that that question is asked of everybody, not in *Olam Habah*, the World-to-Come, but in *Olam Hazeh* (this world). That was the question that was asked to me when I stood in front of the *Kosel*, all by myself, for those two hours. And I couldn't answer it. That's why I cried.

Baruch Hashem, I have now lived here in *Eretz Yisroel* for over twenty years, with a loving wife and children, with a long *kapote*, a *shtreimel* and an increasingly white beard. I simply can't give enough thanks to *Hakodesh Baruch Hu*, for His great *chesed* in giving me the ability to see Him, to feel Him, to come closer to Him, and to be part of *Am Yisroel*.

WARMTH ON ICE

Thousands of square miles of flat, barren ice may hold the key to the mysteries of global climate trends. The Antarctic ice sheet is a place hostile to the vital processes of both plants and animals. It offers no nourishment. There is nothing to smell. Gazing around at the horizon, one is encircled by the meeting of sky above and ice below, as if looking out from the center of a giant white disc. Nevertheless, I would learn to make this ice sheet a home with only a tent, thermos, journal, books, and radio transmitter to connect me to humanity. After training for nearly fifteen years in geophysics, I was proud to be chosen as a member of a select international team of scientists whose long-term mission was to link the fossilized climatological records of the permanent ice caps in the northern and southern hemispheres to determine the scale of processes that may contribute to global warming. The search for unadulterated samples drove the team to increasingly remote locations around the globe. As the work progressed, an individual's professional success could be measured in terms of the cumulative number of months spent in the "deep field."

At graduate school some years earlier, I had come into contact with ancient Jewish teachings about life and the universe. I was delighted to learn how these teachings from my own heritage elucidated not only the realities of the external world, but also those of the vast and sometimes daunting internal world. For me, exploration had always been a solitary endeavor; so my Jewish exploration was also, at first, as intellectual and solitary as if I had been alone in the snow laboratory. Gradually, I began to participate in weekly services and to develop a few close relationships in the small Jewish community of my rural New England college town. I observed that, while others were also striving to explore their worlds, participation in the broader community was an integral part of each individual's journey.

Just as a glacial explorer relies on certain essential tools—global positioning systems, radar transmitters, continuum mechanics, microscopes and thermostatistics—I would require a new set of tools—Hebrew and Aramaic, refined methods of analysis and texts—to pursue my internal journey. Hence, early in my professional career, I took a one-month leave of absence to study at the Ohr Somayach Yeshiva in Jerusalem. There, I found the tools, although I was remarkably unprepared for their discovery. I attended classes in Jewish law, philosophy and mysticism, and participated in the services, rituals and *davening*. I saw spartan living quarters, Shabbos candle lighting, men dancing together in circles and singing, a strange but uniform dress code, strings hanging from men's waists, and ritual hand washing. These sights and sounds felt foreign and even threatening to me.

I made an entry in my diary questioning my decision to take a whole month off from work—an unprecedented act of courage on my part—and spend it with a bunch of people who were only questionably in reality! I resolved that, if I didn't feel more comfortable in a few days, I would find a more satisfying way to spend the balance of my month in Israel. I also told myself that, in spite of what I observed around me, I could keep my head on my shoulders by meditating and repeating slogans learned in "12-step" meetings to keep myself feeling connected to G-d *in spite* of my "threatening" yeshiva surroundings!

On the other hand, I also heard compelling logical discourses explaining the experiences of my ancestors and deep analyses of the mystical dimensions of the world, my perceptions of it, and my perceptions of my true self. The words and melodies that I heard resonated deeply within me. For the first time in my life, I was connecting with something that seemed both spiritually beneficial and consistent with my nascent awareness of myself as a Jew. I decided that I would persevere, one day at a time, despite my agitation and my urge to flee back to the familiar world outside of the yeshiva. An honest self-assessment revealed that the spiritual grounding that I was beginning to sense was more transcendent and eternal than the competing internal voices of skepticism that urged me to resist change. As I persevered, agitation was slowly complemented by moments of calm, uncanny familiarity, and finally pure joy.

The end of my visit at the yeshiva drew to a close. I was urged to stay longer, but my commitments to my work and my faithful Labrador retriever drew me home. Nonetheless, it was strangely clear to me that my heart would not be full without drawing myself into the world of the yeshiva. It seemed to be the source of the grounded feelings and general "rightness" that I had experienced.

I could not even envision trading in my Birkenstocks for a black yarmulke, or being married to an Orthodox woman, but my heart was open to whatever wisdom and warmth I could absorb.

The day before my departure arrived, as hard as it had been to participate in the yeshiva's activities, it was even harder to leave. How would I keep up the connection to the wisdom and the warmth after I return to New England? That was a question for the rabbis! I approached Rabbi Dovid Gottlieb on the eve of my departure. This required some courage, because I had silently attended Rabbi Gottlieb's lectures and was in awe of his intellect and forceful personality. He graciously welcomed me into his office and we spoke for two hours. His ability to actively listen conveyed a depth of personality that I had never before encountered. I admired his warmth and presence so much that I heard a voice inside me say, "I want to do whatever that Rabbi did, so I can have as much depth of character as he has."

Rabbi Gottlieb implicitly understood that I would return to deep spiritual isolation in rural New England (ironically, I would have called it fulfilling, bucolic and peaceful, before I was introduced to real spirituality at the yeshiva). "How far away do you live from Boston?" he asked. "About a three-hour drive," He wrote down a telephone number and passed me a piece of paper. "When you get back to the States, call this number. It's the telephone number of the Bostoner Rebbe."

The next day, I returned to the States. As soon as I got my bearings, the morning after my arrival, I called the number and Rabbi Naftali Horowitz, the Bostoner Rebbe's son, answered the phone. "Oh. We just received a fax from Rabbi Gottlieb. He said that you would be calling. The Rebbe is not going to be here this Shabbos, but you should come the following Shabbos." O.K. Great. I would come the following Shabbos.

The following Shabbos, I overcame more fear of the unknown, and entered the small Chassidic enclave of the Bostoner Rebbe in Brookline, Massachusetts, only about five miles from the house in which I had grown up. During services on Shabbos morning, I understood virtually nothing. I saw people dressed in Chassidic garb. I had no idea where they had come from. I was repeatedly surprised when one of them would speak to me in English. The Rebbe himself wore a gold-striped Yerushalmi robe and a silver-decorated *tallis*. He had a long, soft white beard.

I soon learned that I had to stand as close to the front as possible to keep track of what was going on. From that vantage point, I was also able to observe and hear the Rebbe. At one point, the Rebbe led the *davening*. When I first heard his voice *davening*, it stirred something inside me. I immediately recognized that the same internal registers that had resonated in Jerusalem were now resonating with the Rebbe's voice. This was the real thing: a connection to the same wisdom and warmth that I had experienced in Jerusalem.

At the end of Shabbos, I had a private meeting with the Rebbe. I told the Rebbe a little bit about myself. The Rebbe then invited me "for Shabbos." Since I was already there and it was already Shabbos, I was quite confused. I responded with a polite, but perfunctory "Thank you." The Rebbe smiled and explained, "No. I mean: *whenever* it's Shabbos, you should be here."

I said, "But, I'll have to drive over three hours each way every week. I don't have the energy for that kind of driving. It would kill me." The Rebbe said, "Don't talk that way or you will talk yourself out of it. From now on, it will be the rule, rather than the exception, that you should be here for Shabbos." Incredulous that I could actually follow through, I agreed. Obviously the Rebbe knew more than I did; and, indeed, for the next fourteen months, Shabbos in Brookline, staying with the Rebbe or his neighbors, was the rule rather than the exception.

Notwithstanding the Rebbe's rule, other more dissonant and contradictory voices continued to compete within me. I had already agreed to participate in expeditions near both geographic poles. Under the rigors of ice-camp life, however, it would be virtually impossible to adhere to my newfound dietary restrictions. It would be even more challenging to begin a day of rest at sundown on Friday in a land where the sun would not set for months. An agitated voice successfully urged me to advance my scientific agenda, negotiate field logistics and board a military ski-equipped plane. A more patient, confident and knowing voice would remain quiet until I was ready to listen. I went off to Antarctica for six weeks.

From a high plateau, the gigantic West Antarctic Ice Sheet creeps slowly but inexorably down a shredded, gravelly, frozen slope to the sea. The deep rumbling of the ice sheet, like a warning beacon, was the rallying call of our scientific mission. Should lubricating meltwater be provided to its base by global warming, the ice could slide catastrophically into the ocean, raising the sea level and changing the face of the Earth in a thunderous geological instant. Standing atop the ice sheet, I had to make an honest assessment of the consequences should I fail to heed the equally deep rumbling that had grown within myself. I evaluated my academic accomplishments and early professional successes, and surmised that I was well positioned to succeed in my field. Yet, at that moment, it also became poignantly clear that my success would lead me far from the wholeness and clarity of purpose that I had begun to sense in Jerusalem. I recognized that I needed to overcome my fear of uncharted internal territory. As if emanating from the straining bed of the ice sheet, thousands of meters below my feet, the knowing voice now directed me to make my next expedition an inner journey.

From Antarctica I returned to New England and resumed my weekly Shabbos trips to Boston, where I had begun to meet many people in the community. I met rabbis and college students who had spent time studying in yeshiva. I was deeply impressed by their intelligence, character, practicality and capacity for caring. It was time to act on my Antarctic realization. I slowly but deliberately plotted a course of action. I set my sights on the Ohr Somayach Yeshiva in Monsey, New York. Although studying in Jerusalem was naturally more attractive, I felt that I could concentrate better if I could more easily fulfill family and professional obligations in the States (and it would be easier to endure the impending separation from my loyal yellow Labrador retriever). I also arranged to gradually complete my research-writing commitments in New York, while I began my encounter with the written and oral traditions of Jewish law.

At the yeshiva in Monsey, I learned about the laws of marriage, acting as an agent, loans and the settling of financial disputes. I learned about the detailed laws of Jewish observances, dietary restrictions, holidays and day-to-day obligations. I closely observed more highly developed fathers, mothers, and children in their religious homes. I was regularly invited to their homes for Shabbos meals, to their weddings, and to other real-life events - apparently they also held by the Rebbe's Shabbos rule! Virtually every Friday night, I had the honor of hearing the *Kiddush* of a Polish grandfather who had survived numerous concentration camps during the Holocaust. His *Kiddush* spoke of a deep personal relationship with the transcendent. It was a *Kiddush* beyond place and time.

In Monsey, I observed sensitivity and wisdom, sorrow and joy. My commitment to an observant way of life strengthened; and I very much wanted to achieve a degree of mastery in this new discipline, comparable to that which I had achieved in the physics of snow and ice. Painfully, I was forced to accept that my discovery had occurred too late in life for me to become a professional student of Talmud. If I wanted to get married and support a family, I'd have to make use of my existing scientific skills in a way more conducive to both a traditional lifestyle and disciplined Jewish study.

With the cognitive dissonance that attends all major transitions, and fully realizing that opening an office in New York with a sign reading "Snow Physicist" over the door was unlikely to pay the bills, I strove to extract the essence of my geophysics career, searching for a new application for my skills. I began to redefine myself as a technical commentator and, after much thought and discussion, I decided to explore intellectual property law. I suspected that my skills would guide me through a smooth transition and into an exciting and satisfying new career.

My suspicion was correct. A patent law firm, in need of a technical advisor in oil exploration, agreed. Soon I was working full time and going to law school at night. Now, with the prospect of being able to support a family, the next step was to find a partner in the new life unfolding before me. Not long after, an Ohr Somayach rabbi with whom I had become close, suggested a *shidduch* with a young lady from New England who could share my appreciation of brisk fall mornings with frosted foliage, walks in the woods and sea-kayaking along the coast of Maine. She, too, had listened to her internal voices and had developed a strong desire to grow in the ways of our forefathers. Months later we were married, and we now feel fortunate to be part of the process of building a new Jewish home.

In New York City, city blocks of concrete and steel are replete with mysteries of technological, corporate and sheer human wonder. During the day, I apply my technical skills at the law firm and stretch myself intellectually as I learn to view technology through a legal lens. I also sharpen the tools of my personal discovery and acquire new ones with the help of a Gemara tutor. On Shabbos, I delight in making *Kiddush* for my wife in the warmth of my own home and pour my heart into songs that resonate from the deeply grounded connection that was awakened in Jerusalem. Although I have moments of nostalgia for the ice, the frigid and barren—but awesome—Antarctic ice sheet seems far away from my home today. Instead, I feel nourished by the flow of wisdom and warmth that comes from learning Torah from those who can see beyond the horizon.

THE ROAD BACK TO SINAI

*"When the Jews stood at Mt. Sinai, their impurity
ceased..."*
*Rav Aha the son of Rava asked Rav Ashi: What
about gerim (who were not at Sinai)? He replied:
Although they were not there physically, they were
there spiritually.*

Shabbos 146a

I f becoming a baal teshuvah is a journey towards discovering one's very deepest self, for a *ger tzeddek* the road is particularly long, stretching all the way back to Sinai. So much is hidden; and the task of bringing back these precious sparks to their rightful place is arduous indeed. So much in this world can seem happenstance; and only at the end can one see the guiding Hand that for over three thousand years never once loosened its grasp until success was achieved. As the Chassidic Master Reb Dovid Lelover once said, when Shaul Hamelech was wandering on the way, he didn't need Shmuel Hanavi to tell him where to go (to find his donkeys) but rather where he had really been (en route to greatness).

THE BALANCING ACT

The finals of the National Science Fair Contest were meant to be glamorous peak experiences, and for Renee they were, although not quite in the way intended. They marked the boundary between her one-track careerism and a more complicated balancing of human priorities.

The laboratory tours, the presentations, the visit to the Oval Office, the personal congratulations of the President and the grand awards banquet were all designed to encourage future careers in science, although all that glitter was unnecessary for Renee, who had already decided on a career as a research mathematician. What changed her life was the discovery that her fellow finalists were not equally single-minded about their specialties. Their intellectual interests were broad, extending to literature, natural science, philosophy and history, at all levels far beyond the standard high school curriculum.

Not one to be outdone, Renee came home determined to begin her own personal Great Books program. Now that her college application had finally been submitted, she had eight months until the fall, to learn what great minds throughout the ages had to say about "the meaning of life." She was only sixteen, and that seemed quite enough.

Always methodical, Renee began with Plato and Aristotle and began to work her way through the main philosophers at the rate of one book apiece. In parallel, she applied a similar system to the Western literature. The literature was enjoyable, but the philosophy was disturbing. It was not just that Hegel was torture and Kant obscure; rather their arguments were simply not convincing.

Renee's maternal grandparents were farmers from the Midwest, and she had attended Bible classes in her mother's Presbyterian church. During her summers on the farm, Renee admired the temperance, tradition and respect for elders still found in her grandparent's community. Her mother's family was proud of its pioneer ancestors and their descent from President Zachary Taylor's brother. When she found out that her father was descended from James Monroe, however, she promptly switched her allegiance, and read up on the role of the Monroe Doctrine in American history. Her father, although Protestant by birth, was an avowed atheist and did not attend church with the rest of the family.

When she was four, her father, then a college professor, had taught in India, where she became conscious of the common humanity of all mankind. When Renee became twelve, she rejected Presbyterian theology; she also consciously rejected the streak of xenophobia, including outright anti-Semitism, found in the rural farm outlook.

When her family finally, together, joined a Unitarian church, that stressed liberal values and downplayed religion, she welcomed the change.

Pushing Renee to academic success had been a family project. Her mother, a college teacher, had taught her to read and add when she was four. Renee had inherited her interest in mathematics from her maternal grandmother, the first college-educated woman in her rural community. Grandmother kept her ahead of her class in arithmetic all though elementary school. When she was sixteen, her father casually observed, "Of course you will get your Ph.D."

Once she started her freshman year at college, Renee set aside her personal quest for a sound philosophical basis for life. Perhaps her philosophy class, next semester, would make it all clear. Meanwhile, always competitive, she piled on courses, so she could have a semester free, later, for research.

A senior headed to Princeton for graduate school once explained to her grandly, "For algebraic geometry, Harvard is the place; but for anything else, Princeton is best." Since Princeton's graduate school did not then admit women in mathematics, Renee decided, on the spot, to go to Harvard in algebraic geometry. She soon worked out a program for getting Highest Honors, a program which had her eating breakfast as soon as the dining hall opened and then going straight to the library to study physics.

Over the summer, Renee was a counselor in a summer math program for high-school students, but she had hours to spare for hooking a rug and again pondering the meaning of life. Whereas religious people were troubled by the problem of evil, she, as a non-religious person, was troubled by the "problem of good." She had strongly felt that lying, cheating, stealing and betrayal were wrong, but none of her humanist philosophies provided an adequate foundation for such morality. In desperation, she bought some books by theologians, and tried those. The new school year brought her no closer to a solution.

One day she was sitting in the dining hall across from a Jewish friend, one of the few who observed some semblance of dietary restrictions. To express her pique at some remark, Renee dipped a string bean in ice cream and ate it. No reaction. She dipped a French fry in ice cream and ate it. Still no reaction. She dipped a piece of steak in ice cream and ate it. "Ugh!" the friend protested. That intrigued her. Why did dietary laws produce such an ingrained reaction, when many more rational ethical precepts often sat so lightly on those who purported to hold them?

That weekend some high-school friends were visiting, while Renee was cooking ham and eggs for breakfast. "Listen," asked Debby, "could you leave out the ham in mine?" Another friend added diffidently, "I wasn't planning to say anything but, as long as Debby mentioned it, could you leave it out of mine, too?" Now Renee was really surprised. She had never seen the slightest hint of religiosity in either guest. Whatever the meaning behind the Jewish dietary laws, they certainly had staying power.

Renee decided to experiment with keeping some version of Jewish dietary laws, while declaring firmly that this was not connected to any religious belief. She had two reasons for trying out *kashrut*. One was that, in her despair at finding some obvious, rational basis for morality, she was willing to check out less rational methods, if they seemed to work. The other reason was more future-oriented.

Marrying and raising a family was one of the most important things Renee expected to do with her life, although she didn't intend to let it interfere with her career. Publicly she was planning to marry at twenty-eight, after living independently for two or three years after getting her Ph.D. Privately, she was willing to be bargained down to twenty-six by a strong candidate. A "strong candidate" in her universe was a Phi Beta Kappa *summa cum laude* Ph.D. from

Harvard or the equivalent thereof. As she looked over the field, it was obvious that many of those candidates were going to be Jewish.

Renee didn't believe in split-religion intermarriages. She and her brother had had enough identity problems when her mother had been Presbyterian and her father, atheist. She had been relieved when the entire family became Unitarian. Since she had no strong religious identification of her own, she had always intended to convert to her future husband's religion and raise their children with a single religious identity. She now realized that, if that religion were to be Judaism, then to convert—in the thoroughgoing fashion to which she was accustomed—would require considerable investment. So Renee spent the spring semester keeping pseudo-kosher. Since there was no one to invite her to a Passover *seder*, she spent all eight days eating nothing but what the college provided: *matzah*, cream cheese and jelly. For the next twenty years, Renee was unable to look at cream cheese and jelly spread on *matzah*, much less eat it.

When Renee arrived home for her summer vacation, her mother made the family one of Renee's favorite meals: pork chops with mashed potatoes and sauerkraut. Her experiment in keeping kosher had only been intended for the school year. However, as she faced that platter of pork chops, she realized that she simply couldn't eat them. She was forced to try explaining her behavior to her parents, while she still had trouble explaining it to herself. Her excuse was plausible, but not the whole truth.

She again spent the summer as a counselor, but this time one of her fellow counselors, Janet, was from an Orthodox family who knew a lot about keeping kosher. Renee learned that "shortening" on a food label meant "lard" and what the "O-U" stood for. She found out about hand-washing. Janet started to teach her the Hebrew "*aleph-beis*" from a Telma soup poster, and they went together to Friday night services at the local Hillel, which had an Orthodox Rabbi. They both fasted on the fast days, and Renee began to learn

Hebrew. Janet also didn't ride or turn on lights on Shabbos, but Renee wasn't up to that yet—although she didn't do mathematics on Shabbos.

Back in school for the fall semester, Renee attended synagogue occasionally. This brought her some acquaintance with the Torah readings, which she struggled to follow with her limited Hebrew, but it also brought her square up against the problem of the existence of G-d.

During winter vacation, her parents' church had a "Students' Day," when returning college students would talk about their experiences. Renee asked to be one of the speakers. The freshmen spoke first; they seemed to have no particular interest in maintaining any religious affiliation at college. Renee, at her own request, had been slated last.

"We were given a religious education," she said, "which was intended to teach us tolerance. We were taken to a mosque, to a Catholic church, to a synagogue. Underneath it all, however, was the message that religion was a crutch, that faith was not for our day and age, that intelligent, rational people did not believe in G-d. Not only is this not religion, it is not even *tolerance*." She described, in brief, her own continuing spiritual search and concluded, "I am interested in what religion has to offer, I might even be ready to believe in G-d, but I think you have made that impossible for me."

Her speech had immediate and drastic repercussions. First, the director of the religious education program, a sincerely religious Unitarian minister's widow resigned, saying, "She is right. It was not for results like this that I undertook the job." Then the minister resigned, saying that he had been having doubts lately about his calling to the ministry. He thought, perhaps, that he would go into social work instead. Finally, Renee asked herself: Who were these people to decide whether or not she could believe in G-d?

• • •

Renee spent her spring semester doing research in Germany. There, among the shards of the remaining Jewish community, she spent her first Passover *seder* and attended her first circumcision ceremony (*bris*). The *mohel*, imported from England for the occasion, asked her if she was planning to convert. When she said that she thought she was, he explained to her about the laws of the Sabbath, and she started being more careful about riding, carrying or turning on lights.

When she got back to the States, she checked out Reform, Conservative and Orthodox conversions, finally settling on Conservative, which seemed the closest to where she was holding. The Conservative rabbi asked what commitments the Orthodox rabbi had expected from her.

"*Kashrus*, Shabbos and the laws of family purity," Renee answered. He had given her a pamphlet on the latter subject that she had read with interest, although she hadn't yet made up her mind. She would have liked to speak to someone who actually did this.

"Ha!" expostulated the rabbi. "Ask him if his wife keeps it!"

Renee was confused by this remark, since the Orthodox rabbi had seemed quite sincere. She was even more confused when she actually went to the *mikvah* in Brooklyn to meet the Conservative rabbi for her conversion. The *mikvah* was a large building with many rooms. It surely wasn't supported just by an occasional conversion. Who did use it if, as the Conservative rabbi had insinuated, the wives of Orthodox rabbis did not?

By this time, Mr. Strong Candidate had appeared, with all the necessary qualifications except that his Ph.D. was still in the future. However, Jonathan had no intention at all of waiting around until Renee was twenty-six, and questioned how many other candidates of the sort she wanted would still be unmarried by then. Since "strong candidates" were now also expected to be Jews interested in being observant, this argument was decisive, and she agreed to get married, not only before her Ph.D., but even before finishing her Bachelor's degree.

Her grandmother was dubious about Renee getting married at age twenty. Both she and Renee's mother had gotten married in their thirties.

"Don't worry, Grandma," Renee hastened to assure her, "I'm still going to get my Ph.D."

"There's many a slip twixt the cup and the lip," quavered Grandma darkly.

In the meantime, Renee had been clued in by Ruthie, the Israeli wife of one of the Hillel regulars, that the laws of family purity were indeed kept by Orthodox Jews, and Renee was already learning them. Ruthie was also teaching her Hebrew.

"Are you really thinking of moving to Israel?"

"Yes, we are," Renee told her. "It seems to us that Israel has more effect on the Diaspora than the Diaspora has on Israel. If we want to be at the center of things Jewishly, that's where we should go."

A line appeared between Ruthie's brows, and she said slowly, "If you are serious about living in Israel, I think you should try to get a letter from an Orthodox rabbi saying that your conversion is valid. When my husband and I wanted to get married, he had to get all sorts of documents from his rabbi in Switzerland to prove that he was unmarried and Jewish. Your children might have trouble when they come to get married."

Jonathan, himself just sliding over from right-wing Conservative to left-wing Orthodox under the influence of Harvard Hillel, traveled out to Brookline to speak to the Bostoner Rebbe. Jonathan arrived at the Rebbe's office. First he cleared up some questions about the laws pertaining to marriage that had come out of his studies in the *Mishnah*. Then, right at the end, he dropped the bombshell about Renee's Conservative conversion.

The Rebbe explained gently that they ought to do better than that. He suggested that Renee try to find an Orthodox rabbi near where she was living who would be willing to convert her. A family with whom she had spent Shabbos sent her to their local rabbi with a warm recommendation. He asked her a few questions to ascertain her level of observance and knowledge.

"How long do you wait after hard cheese?"

"I wait six hours after eating meat before eating anything *milchig*, but I only wait an hour between milk and meat. No one ever told me that hard cheese is different."

"We wait six hours after hard cheese too. What blessing do you say on a banana?"

"I say the blessings before and after bread, but I'm not really up to all the other blessings yet."

The rabbi looked down at his steepled fingers for a moment or two and then looked up again at Renee. "No, I don't think I can do this conversion. Perhaps, if you do get married anyway, you can come back and ask me again afterwards."

"But if I converted again, then I would also have to get married again," protested Renee.

"True, you would," said the rabbi with a shrug.

Renee gave up on trying to get an Orthodox conversion, and phoned Jonathan to tell him as much. She knew that he was very worried by the whole problem, but it didn't seem to her that she was going to find an Orthodox rabbi who, knowing about her engagement, would be willing to convert her, and she certainly wasn't interested in a conversion obtained under false pretenses.

Some days later, Jonathan called her back. "The Rebbe found an Orthodox Beit Din willing to deal with your case. You have to be in Boston on Thursday at ten."

Renee was in Boston by ten on Thursday to begin the process. When it was finally completed, she was very relieved. And eventually she and Jonathan were married.

• • •

Renee's conversion was not the only thing that had to be done over. One day a fellow Hillel member, Kenny, commented that he was driving out to Brookline to *toivel* some new glass dishes in the *mikvah*. This reminded Jonathan that, when he had set up his own kosher kitchen, he hadn't known a thing about immersing dishes.

"Can I bring some too?" he asked anxiously.

"Sure!" answered Kenny, not knowing that, when packed up, the dishes to which Jonathan was referring would fill seven or eight cartons.

Another time, Jonathan came home to find Renee crying and dropping bottles into the trashcan. Worcester sauce, sniff, plunk. Chutney, sniff, plunk. Horseradish, sniff, plunk.

"What happened? What are you doing?"

"I'm doing teshuva," sobbed Renee, "for buying all these things which could contain wine vinegar and don't have any *kashrus* supervision."

That summer they stayed in Jerusalem for two months, trying to see what it would be like to live there. When they first arrived, the manager of the small student hostel where they spent the first night gave Renee a pamphlet about the laws of modesty. Both she and Jonathan were offended, particularly since, in those days of mini-skirts, Renee's knee-length skirts were considered pretty conservative.

A few weeks later, on a bus, she ran into Shelley, one of their Shabbos guests from Hillel. She was wearing thick stockings and a long-sleeved print dress. "What's this?" Renee asked.

"I was 'adopted' by a family in Mea Shearim," Shelley explained.

Back in the States, over the course of that fall, Renee "converted" her wardrobe as well. Since they were eking out a meager existence on their graduate student stipends, she sewed most of the clothes for her new "maxi" look. These were the Vietnam War years; but Jonathan got a draft deferment as a rabbinical student by studying— five nights a week and Sundays—at a yeshiva run by the Bostoner Rebbe's son, Rabbi Mayer Horowitz, in Brookline. He continued his doctoral studies in the daytime. For Jonathan, it was a welcome opportunity to make up the Jewish background he missed.

Renee herself lagged far behind him in Jewish knowledge. Her efforts were confined to learning Hebrew and studying the laws of Shabbos. She had no problems with practicing everything to the best of her ability; she had committed herself at her conversion to keeping the *mitzvos*, and it was a matter of personal integrity that she should do so. She had liberated herself from her Unitarian upbringing sufficiently to be *willing* to believe in G-d, and that did usually seem the best explanation for Jewish history. However, she also sometimes doubted whether her beliefs were really true. When this happened, she would sit down and try to work things out again from the beginning.

Given all these changes, had Renee finally realized the futility of worldly ambitions and given up on getting her Highest Honors and her Ph.D.? Well, not exactly. She spent all her daytime hours in the library and she indeed graduated with the coveted *Summa* line on her bachelor's diploma. She had gotten into Harvard and studied algebraic geometry, just as she had planned. As for the doctorate, since Jonathan was two years older, she decided to get her degree in three years so that they could look for jobs at the same time. They had not yet, unfortunately, had any children, which made that more practical; and the preliminary draft of her thesis was approved by winter of her third year.

Renee and Jonathan were walking home from Hillel one Friday night with their Shabbos guest, Bob, when a car turned left and almost ran them down. They jumped out of the way and were still looking after this first car in indignation when they heard a squeal of brakes. Renee was knocked up onto the hood of a second car and slid down onto the road, while the two men were just bruised.

As Renee lay on the pavement, her first thought was to hope that she would not now be run over by yet a third car. Her second thought was, "Well, I'm glad I wasn't killed before I got my Ph.D.!"

They did graduate together, when Jonathan was twenty-five and Renee twenty-three. Both got university positions in Israel, in the Tel Aviv area, and they bought an apartment in Bnei Brak. This brought a new string of changes. Jonathan began learning the Talmud in depth and began teaching a class for university students as well. Renee was introduced to Rashi's commentary on the Torah and the Prophets...and ran smack into her old philosophical difficulties.

One day she was reading at home, her baby asleep in another room. She opened her book to the beginning, and found that the first commandment was "to believe that G-d exists, as it is written, 'I am Hashem your G-d.'" Renee felt herself under terrible pressure. She had committed herself to keeping the commandments, but what is the meaning of a commandment to believe? She surely behaved *as if* she believed in G-d, but did she really? On the other hand, the idea of doubting G-d to His very face, as it were, was terribly embarrassing. Renee rose from her chair, took her prayer book, and began to pray the afternoon service with tears running down her cheeks. When she got to the blessing, "Hear our voice!" she added the special section for confession, "Please, O G-d, I have sinned..." for her moments of disbelief. She finished the prayer, kissed the book, and returned to her studying.

A couple of years later, when Jonathan had gotten rabbinical ordination and was about to do his army service as an army rabbi,

Renee was finally ready to face the question whether there was a conflict between her university job and her Orthodox worldview. Jonathan had asked a similar question of the Bostoner Rebbe, when he visited Israel, and had been told to stay at the university where he could affect students with whom no other Orthodox Jews had contact. Since the Rebbe was not available, Jonathan, in his army uniform, took her to Rav Shach, the Ponevezh Rosh Yeshiva, one of the best known and most highly respected Torah scholars of the generation. He explained to the Rav their various considerations.

Rav Shach simply asked him, "Do you have a television in your home?"

"G-d forbid!" answered Jonathan.

"Then it shouldn't do any harm if she keeps her university job," he answered, with a gentle smile.

For years Renee had been afraid to ask this question, one she had long kept bottled up inside. Now that she had gotten the "easy" answer, it was almost a disappointment. There was a certain appeal to the idea of making a dramatic sacrifice for her faith. Now her long-time conflict would have no simple or simplistic resolution. She would have to spend the rest of her life constantly balancing priorities.

• • •

Note: Renee and Jonathan are still living and working as professors in Israel. Jonathan also teaches a daily Talmud class and lectures to the general public. Most of their children are not married. Renee has published several popular Jewish novels and two non-fiction books on the Holocaust under her well-known pen-name. Every year, usually around Rosh Hashanah, they wonder again if there is some way they could reorganize their lives that would do more for the Jewish people.

‿◌‿

DESPITE IT ALL

I grew up in West Virginia in a relatively assimilated Lebanese-American family. My grandparents were all born in Lebanon and Syria. They continued to speak Arabic to each other after decades in America, still worshiped at the Syrian Orthodox church, socialized with other uprooted Lebanese and ate primarily Middle-Eastern food. My parents, in their desire to assimilate, were very successful business entrepreneurs and members of a classy country club. They attended the First Presbyterian Church and sent me to Wellesley College.

I attended the Presbyterian church most Sundays willingly, but it was a dry experience. I had no question about the existence of G-d, but had no idea how to relate to him. I went to a weeklong conference on prayer when I was fourteen hoping to learn how to create a dialogue with G-d, and came away confused and disinterested. Whenever I could I would go to the Syrian Orthodox church with my grandparents. I didn't understand the Arabic; but I was enthralled by the richness of the ritual, the chanting and the incense. I felt something akin to spirituality that I had no way of understanding at the time.

I left home when I was sixteen to live in Sweden for a year. I had the distinct feeling that something was missing in my life, but I didn't have a clue what it was. When I was seventeen, during my first year at Wellesley, I learned to meditate. I felt that I was tuning into something spiritual, something beyond the material. It was a feeling that deeply attracted me. During the next six-year period, I lived for a year in France studying at the Sorbonne, and I spent two years in Italy and Spain studying meditation with Maharishi Mahesh Yogi.

By the time I started graduate school to study psychology, I was totally entrenched in an inner journey searching for psychological and spiritual growth. I often spent two hours a day meditating and felt that that time of expansion, in which I was building a larger perspective on life, was the foundation of my life. I established a relationship with Michael, a Jew, who is now my husband, while we were in grad school. He took a meditation course that I taught, and afterwards we often went away to weekend meditation retreats.

We spent seven years in Vermont as practicing psychologists. In the beginning, we maintained a great deal of involvement in meditation. As the years went by, and we became more and more ensconced in our professional life, the work hours grew and the meditation hours decreased. Finally one day, as Michael was on a 10-mile run and I was accompanying him on my bicycle, we realized that our lives had become seriously off balance.

We had attained the American dream. We lived in a big beautiful house, had two cars, nice vacations, thriving psychology practices, professional status and recognition and dear friends. We should have been on top of the world. However, we were both aware that there had to be something more to life. We knew that something was missing and were pretty sure that it had to do with spirituality. We sensed that we had lost perspective on life and had been hypnotized by the *status quo*, a value system we found lacking. On the spot we decided that we had to take drastic action to save our souls, and we immediately formulated a plan.

We decided to shut down our current lives and to throw ourselves out to the world to regain an understanding of what was important. We asked the "powers that be," our euphemism for G-d, to lead us to what was missing and inform us what we were supposed to be doing with our lives. This was clearly an articulated prayer, although we didn't speak about "prayer" in those days. Instead, we referred to it as "having clear intention," or as "looking to the universal intelligence for guidance."

Three months later we found ourselves leaving the airport in Brussels, on our newly outfitted bicycles, to launch a trip around the world. Our itinerary was to go wherever we would be led. We had no doubt that we would be led. And we were.

While traveling on our bikes through Europe, including transversing the Alps, we had many wonderful adventures. We were invited countless times into people's homes, wined and dined, and almost always given some indication of where our next stop was supposed to be. The environment educated us, and we listened as carefully as possible to the messages. Whenever we tried to initiate a next logical move from our side, such as living in a monastery, volunteering in a meditation center, and so on, our plans never worked out. When we relinquished control and followed whatever instructions we were given, things flowed along in total harmony.

From Europe we went to Lebanon to visit my distant cousins. They received us with open arms and treated us royally, while they explained to us that all the problems of the Lebanese were due to the Jews. Their version of the relevant facts was that Jewish refugees from Europe displaced the Palestinians who in turn wreaked havoc in Lebanon. There was no question that they were suffering. They lived in constant fear for their safety and their environs was destroyed by fighting between the various Palestinian factions who had set up headquarters in Beirut. Although we could empathize with their problems, it was intolerable to hear such comments from them as, "the world would have been better, if Hitler had finished his job properly."

Our next stop was Israel, where we loosely planned to volunteer on a kibbutz for a month or so and then continue on to Africa. Israel welcomed us from the first day with a variety of experiences that took our breath away and raised many questions.

We spent our first nights with Arabs in Acco, who told us "The walls have ears," and refused to discuss politics. Then we stayed with a secular Jew in Ma'alot who spoke at length about the school children who had been murdered there and her resulting mistrust and hatred of Arabs. Our next visit was to Kibbutz Sasa where we were inundated with anti-religious rhetoric. We then found our way to Tzefat where we stayed with a Modern Orthodox Jew who was vehement in his criticism of "Ultra-Orthodox" Jews. Afterwards we stayed at Kibbutz Ein Gev and realized that kibbutz life was actually not what we were looking for. We stayed at a convent in Nazareth while we visited all the Christian sites and enjoyed the Arab food of my childhood. While visiting one large church, we inadvertently got caught in the middle of a communion service, which left me cold, and made Michael extremely anxious. We arrived in Tel Aviv, but couldn't leave that inferior copy of New York quickly enough.

The day we finally started out for Jerusalem, climbing the highway eastward from Tel Aviv, the wind was blowing so fiercely down the mountain that we couldn't continue. Although we had been through extremely difficult weather and high mountains in Europe, this was the first time on our whole trip that we had to turn around because the riding was simply too hard. The wind blew us to an intersection where we saw a sign for Kfar Chabad, and we recognized the name from someone we had met in Tzefat. Having no other place calling us at the moment, we decided to land there. We arrived at dusk on Yud-Tet b'Kislev, the date of the first Lubavitcher Rebbe's release from prison in Czarist Russia. The entire village was out in the streets, singing and dancing in the light of torches, as they celebrated bringing a new Torah scroll to the synagogue. In some incomprehensible way, I felt overwhelmingly that I had "come home."

We were invited to stay with a wonderful family, who took us under their wings and started to introduce us to Judaism. This couple had the capacity to answer all our questions in a profound and broad-based way that was both satisfying and challenging. One evening the wife asked me to do her a favor and pick up a book that she had accidentally left in the synagogue. It was only the third time in my life that I had been in a synagogue.

The first time was when I was about twelve years old. I had long been vaguely aware of the local Conservative synagogue mostly as a place that was different and off-limits in some strange way. I had visited all the churches of my friends, but had never been invited by my Jewish friends to accompany them to synagogue. At the end of the year, all the Girl Scout troops in the city held their final ceremony there. I remember being very excited about entering the building and feeling awestruck by being in what I experienced as a holy place.

While in graduate school, friends invited Michael and me to go with them to their Conservative synagogue on Yom Kippur. Michael was not particularly interested, but I insisted. We walked in at some point in the afternoon. People were milling around and being generally inattentive. We sat down on some folding chairs by the edge, and again I felt awestruck. I had no idea what was going on, but I again had the same clear experience of being near something holy. After an hour or so, they all wanted to leave; but I couldn't pull myself away. I didn't understand what the attraction was; but I knew that there was something there that felt right to be close to.

So there I was in Kfar Chabad, Israel, about to enter a synagogue for the third time. I stood for a moment outside in my sandals (the only shoes I had) in the freezing rain, shivering and very frightened. I couldn't move. This was not typical behavior for me. With my heart pounding, I opened the door of the empty, cold building and climbed the stairs to the women's section. I could barely breathe. I tiptoed to the front of the balcony and stood with the shul in front of me. I could sense the walls shimmering in the iridescent light. I was overcome with an immense shame and humility, and felt that I had to hide my eyes. I felt terrified to face G-d, whose presence was magnificently before me. I could only cry. Not soft tears, but heaving, breathtaking sobs. Years of longing were pouring out of me. I was bombarded with unexpected images: holocaust suffering, feeling the burden of the world's needs on top of me, feeling responsible to do something (although I didn't know what), feeling accountable for my life and somehow for *Am Yisrael*. Pure raw experience that made no rational sense. Just something that jumped out and grabbed me. After a long while, when I could catch my breath, I fled, for I didn't know what else to do.

We eventually made our way to Jerusalem where we stayed with an irreverent Israeli whom we had met on a beach in Greece. In the face of his mocking, we planned to sit through a few classes in Judaism in Jerusalem, and then to continue on our journey. After a few classes, we decided to stay for just a few more days. A few days led to a few weeks. After two weeks of the most compelling classes I had ever taken, it was absolutely clear that Michael and I had to break up our relationship with each other. As painful as it was, neither one of us had any doubt that it was the only option. Michael moved into a yeshiva with plans to learn indefinitely.

I moved into a temporary apartment, with plans to take a few more classes and then decide whether to continue the trip by myself. It was a confusing and disorienting time. I loved what I was learning and felt that I could not walk away from it. At the same time, I took the idea of being a Jew very seriously and was not prepared to consider conversion frivolously. Although I knew that I was in no way obligated to do so, I very much wanted to keep the *mitzvos* from the very beginning. After about ten months of learning and keeping *mitzvos*, I started to feel that I was in the right place doing the right thing. I kept feeling that I had come to myself in a way that was more complete than ever before.

I decided to go to the United States to consider converting to Judaism from a fresh perspective. I needed to test whether I was being swept away by the intensity of my experience, or whether I had possibly been brainwashed. My reception in America was extremely negative. My family said that, if I converted, they would disown me. My dearest friends, both Jews and non-Jews (with one exception), believed that I had "gone crazy" and did everything they could to discourage me from becoming Orthodox.

In spite of the rejection and lack of support, I felt more and more strongly that it was the only true option for me. I didn't exactly believe that I wanted to be Jewish; it was more a matter of longing to be as close to G-d as I could be. It seemed clear to me that that was what G-d wanted from me. Even if it meant that I would lose everything else that had been precious to me up to that time, I basically felt that I had no real choice.

I came back to Jerusalem, and spent a great deal of time at the *Kosel*. The feeling of sureness about converting became stronger and stronger, until I finally officially initiated the conversion process. Even though I knew intellectually that the *beis din* would have to turn me away the first two times that I approached them, the procedure was enormously painful. By the time I stood before them, I was certain that I needed to be Jewish, and continuing to live as a non-Jew was becoming disorienting and unacceptable. I felt on the outside of the *mitzvos* when I did them. It was like being outside of existence. It is a very difficult status to describe; but I felt that I was in "Never-Never Land" just waiting to be viable.

When my third meeting with the *beis din* arrived, I was very excited. It was several days before Rosh Hashanah, and I had pushed to be able to get the appointment with them with enough time to convert before the holiday. I was thrilled to be able to enter the new year as a new person. It never occurred to me that they would say no. I couldn't believe what I was hearing.

"You don't know Hebrew well enough yet," they claimed. I wasn't exactly sure whether to laugh or to scream at this. Were they just joking around with me?

I began to argue with them, "I have many Jewish friends in America who don't even know what a *mitzvah* is, and who don't know half the Hebrew I do. What do you mean I need to know Hebrew better to be Jewish?" I was starting to get a bit intense.

The discussion that followed quickly escalated into a heated argument. They actually wanted me to go and learn Hebrew for a year (!) and then come back to them again. As far as I was concerned, this was not an option. The thought of not becoming Jewish immediately was so unnerving that I was becoming hysterical. I had to make them understand that this was completely out of the question, and that I was not about to stand there and negotiate it with them.

I am normally a person who is very respectful of authority. It is rare for me to voice disagreement. However, I felt so desperate at that moment that it didn't even occur to me that it would be *chutzpadik* for me to refuse to leave until they agreed to convert me. But that's exactly what I did!

They looked at me nonplussed. They tried to convince me to be reasonable. I refused. The more they insisted that I leave, the more I became hysterical, crying, screaming and refusing to move. I think they thought I went crazy, because they said they were sending me to a psychologist. Well, I didn't mind that. I knew my way around that turf quite well!

The psychologist tried to calm me down with every trick in the book. He tried to reason with me that I was making a big deal out of nothing, that it was time for me to settle down and be cooperative. He couldn't understand why it would be such a problem to put things off for a while longer and study Hebrew in an ulpan for a while. After three hours of intense debate, and many phone calls to rabbis that knew me, he agreed to go back to the *beis din* with me and to try to convince them to convert me.

Back we went. Long discussions. Lots of tears. "But don't you know it's a serious thing to be Jewish?" they asked me. "Don't you know that it's much, much easier to be a righteous *goy*?" "Don't you know that the world will hate you?" "Haven't you heard of the Holocaust?" "How would you deal with your own children, G-d forbid, being killed just for being Jewish?" That one slowed me down, I must admit. But only for a second.

"Yes, yes. Even for my life, and even for the life of my children. Please, please make me Jewish now," I implored. More whispered consultations.

Finally, I had gotten through. The head rabbi, leaned down from the dais, eyes softened for the first time, his finger wagging in my face, and whispered, "O.K. Just remember to be a real good Jew."

Two nights later, I stood proudly and calmly listening to *Kiddush* on Rosh Hashanah while my tears flowed. This time they were soft ones.

"Blessed are You, Hashem, who has granted us life, and preserved us and brought us to this time."

TO BE OR NOT TO BE

I'm not sure where a story of spiritual yearning, struggle and progress should properly begin. Perhaps there is no "right" place; but my childhood home in Ohio didn't seem to hold much promise. My father was Episcopalian and my mother was neutral, with a vague touch of Jewish. He was a scientist; she was an artist. My father had been adopted and knew nothing of his biological roots, while my mother had a distinct aversion to genealogy of any kind. Still, when my fifth-grade class had to make family trees, she contributed ten generations! My cousins occasionally hinted at nobility, but my mother typically dismissed her ancestors as "pirates and horse thieves."

I attended the Episcopal church of my father. My earliest recollection of that church was that my mother didn't like it. Eventually, she absolutely refused to go. Why? Because the priest there had delivered an anti-Semitic sermon. "What is anti-Semitism?" I asked. And she told me. Actually, my mother had never been very attached to that church, although she occasionally went to a synagogue on Passover and Rosh Hashanah.

If my religious education was lacking, I did gain a lifelong appreciation for ethics and good deeds. When I was fifteen years old, one of the members of my father's church appealed for money to keep his street-ministry coffee house running in a poor Catholic neighborhood. Eventually he had to close its doors, due to lack of funds. I had a paper route, so I took my money and used it to reopen the coffee house. I soon became its driving force, going out to other teenagers on the street and trying to convince them to "Give G-d a chance." Downtown, during the early '70s, there were Moonies and Hari Krishna types handing out all sorts of religious tracts. I had a few fundamentalist tracts that I handed out. Once, I looked in the gutter and saw some tracts entitled *Be Happy* and *A Voice Calls Out to G-d*. I was curious about which guru had written them and picked one up. To my surprise, it was written by some rabbi, someone called Rabbi Nachman of Breslov.

My best friend was Jewish; and he invited me to go with him to a public *seder* at his Conservative synagogue. I didn't know much about Judaism, so I looked in the Bible. There it said that only circumcised people could eat from the Passover offering. I told mother that I probably couldn't go to the *seder* because I wasn't circumcised. She said that she had something to tell me ... not only was I circumcised, but I was actually a Jew. We were "from the tribe of Judah."

This revelation precipitated a major upheaval in my whole worldview. I started challenging the church's minister about the sources of his traditions, such as his fringed prayer shawl and the ritual washing of his hands before communion. The minister, at first, attempted to find Christian sources; but eventually, chagrined, he had to admit that they came from Judaism. I decided that, from that day on, I was going to try and live as much as possible as a Jew. I started keeping Shabbos and attended a Conservative synagogue as often as I could. Later, when I started college, I was anxious to move out of our home, so I could start keeping kosher.

After about two years of this, my Jewish friend began to become alarmed by the "Episcopalian" who was attending his synagogue. We stopped talking very much. One day the *gabbai* called me up to the Torah for an *aliyah*. I was embarrassed because I couldn't read the blessings in Hebrew, but the *gabbai* assured me that an English transliteration would be available. My heart was pounding. I was thrilled. As I walked up to the *bima*, I thought I would faint. Suddenly my friend jumped up and said, "He cannot go up to the Torah." When the *gabbai* protested, my friend shouted in front of the whole synagogue, "He cannot go up. HE IS NOT JEWISH!"

I was mortified. I turned around to leave. Then I remembered reading in one of my books that it was disrespectful to leave the room when the Torah was being read. So I stood red-faced near the doorway until the reading was over, and then left.

It was time to look in the phonebook for another synagogue. I found one next to an old steel mill. It seemed quite quiet. I walked the two miles there on Shabbos and found that I was the tenth man. I was pleased to be able to help complete and *daven* with a Jewish *minyan*. I was already taking Hebrew classes and, little by little, was learning some of the prayers. All of the men were over 70; none of their children came. It turned out that all of their children had intermarried, and none were interested in coming. Later, the man who stayed behind to lock the doors began turning off all the lights, in violation of the Sabbath. When he saw my surprised look, he joked, "I'm the Shabbos *goy*." My heart dropped. When I found out that another member picked up the rest of the *minyan* from the old folks home in his car, another Sabbath violation, I decided that it was time to find another synagogue.

When I was nineteen, I wore a fisherman's cap and a jeans jacket with a peace symbol. I was once walking down the local Jewish avenue, with my gold wire-rimmed glasses and a scraggly red beard, when a young man in his twenties, wearing a long black coat and a Chassidic hat, spotted me from across the street. He headed straight for me and said that G-d had "lifted him up on angels' wings" to bring him to me. He was collecting money for a new yeshiva in Jerusalem and asked for a donation. I was thrilled to be part of the Jewish people in this special way, so I wrote him a check for $100. He also asked if he and his friends could stay with me in my apartment for a few days, while they collected money for the yeshiva. When they arrived, later that evening, only one spoke a broken English. But they answered all my questions and, every couple minutes, they would form a circle and dance with me in my living room. When I woke the next morning, they had already found my guitar. Although they didn't know one bit how to play, one picked it up and strummed, while we danced some more.

I asked what kind of Jews they were and they said that they were Chassidim—Breslover Chassidim. So, after they left, I tried to find out more about Chassidim. They had also met my girlfriend, and had told me that it is good to get married before twenty. So, one month before my twentieth birthday, I got married.

The only Chassidim in our town, besides a Rebbe who had left twenty years before (my apartment was located in his former home), were Chabad. I had heard of them but I didn't know where they were. One day I was riding my bicycle when a thirty year-old man, with white strings flying from his jeans, went flying past me on his bicycle. He said to me, "Hey Jew boy, why don't you drop by the Chabad House." I asked him where it was and he told me. I finally caught up with him at the office that the local Jewish community had provided to "keep the Chabadniks off the street and to stop them from pestering people about *tefillin* and Shabbos candles." The first thing he asked me was "Is your mother Jewish?"

I thought for a long second, reflecting on the dual life my mother seemed to lead, and hesitantly answered, "yes." He noticed my hesitancy and started to probe me further. He seemed to be saying, "Listen, boy. The minute there is a doubt, you had better get some proof." So, the next time I visited home, I started plying my mother with questions; but she wouldn't answer them. After almost giving up, she finally gave me the name of her great-uncle in Connecticut who was "the family genealogist." I continued to look for one scrap of information about my maternal grandmother or great-grandmother—one slight indication that they had attended a synagogue or had Jewish sounding maiden names. Instead, I kept finding out more about my non-Jewish grandfathers.

Eventually, I pieced together that my mother's grandmother had lived with her husband in the East End of London. She had been a governess in a wealthy home in Elephant-and-Castle; but in 1912, she had another baby and was promptly fired. Not knowing where to turn, the couple accepted the offer of a homestead in Saskachewan, Canada, from the British Government. Although the land was free, they failed miserably as farmers and, in the 1920s, my grandmother became an illegal alien in Los Angeles. I kept saying that I would trade "all the princes in the world" for one rabbi on my mother's side; but none appeared, and all the maiden names I could find were British-sounding.

All this time I was observing *mitzvos* and reading every Jewish book I could find. I went to classes taught by two rabbis, one an elderly Chassid who told wondrous stories, and one a Misnagged who spoke about Jewish theology. When I began to realize that I might not be Jewish at all, I decided to confide everything to my Chabad friend. He sent me to the head of the local Hillel Academy, who laughed at me. Then I went to another rabbi who had no time for me. Finally, I went to the local *beis din*, who tried to talk me out of it. By this time, I was fed up. I had been keeping Shabbos for five years, and had been keeping kosher for three.

Finally I shouted that even if they wouldn't accept me, I would keep Jewish law anyway. The *beis din* warned against it. Perhaps I wasn't Jewish, and a non-Jew who keeps all aspects of Jewish law deserves death. I said that, even so, I would keep it. If I died, I died. What else could I say? Judaism represented everything—the underlying, albeit sometimes obscured, source of everything I knew to be true. With that they seemed to be convinced that I was sincere, and they organized a *geiros lechumra* (a conversion to obviate doubt). They also arranged a second wedding ceremony. Now, whether baal teshuvah or *ger*, all was fixed once and for all. A year later, our first child was born and our young new family made *aliyah* to Israel.

Ending my story there might make for a neat happy ending; but life went on. Several years passed and I lost considerable money by taking out a fixed currency mortgage just before Israel devalued its currency by 20%. Overnight, I became $20,000 in debt. I took a second job, and then a third. I was never home and, eventually, caught between strain and absence, my marriage ended in divorce.

Yet, even then, Hashem, in His great mercy, never deserted me. One night, before the worst consequences of my debt had emerged, a co-worker of mine, stopped by for a visit. She was the genealogist for a well-known synagogue in London. I happened to mention to her that I thought my maternal grandmother was from that area; and my friend asked for her name. I hesitated. What if she wasn't Jewish? Did everybody have to know?

Eventually I told her: Helen Morton. She said, "Oh yes. In fact, her parents were married in our synagogue. They weren't affiliated with the synagogue that much, however. They were quite assimilated, you know." Originally their name was Mortar; and the marriage registry listed them as 'Mr. and Mrs. Mortar, aka Morton.' So I *had* been Jewish after all!

In the 1980s, under the auspices of the Gerrer Rebbe, *shlita*, my business partner and I had begun an innovative computer programming company in Jerusalem. We employed eighteen religious workers, mostly part-time. The kollel wives worked in the morning and the kollel men worked in the afternoon, after their morning *seder*. *Baruch Hashem,* all developed a profession that still benefits them and their families. I sold out to my partner after my divorce; but I still coach several religious Jewish programmers here in Israel. I try to go beyond sharing technical expertise to give them *chizuk* on a personal and spiritual level.

During a visit back to the States, I was *zocheh* to meet the Bostoner Rebbe, *shlita*, and my new, truly Jewish religious life flourished. I remarried and moved back to Jerusalem. The subsequent years have been full of growth—not without their challenges, but based on a firm foundation and filled with hope for the future.

His and Hers

HIS STORY.

Let's face it. One of the hardest parts of being a *ger* or baal teshuvah is the endless questioning of well-meaning people, who forget that, just as they have a right to personal privacy, so do others. Is it uncontrollable curiosity, nervousness, suppressed voyeurism, or misplaced interest? Who knows. But one doesn't give up his right to a private life just because he accepted, rather than inherited, *mitzvah* observance.

Why did I become *frum*? I didn't. I first became Jewish and have been trying to become *frum* ever since. I haven't been too successful; but I have tried, through perhaps not hard enough.

Nor do the questions stop with me. People often ask my wife why her husband became Jewish. She always pointedly answers, "He never saw fit to tell *me*, so I reckoned it was none of *my* business." But they never take the hint. People, aware of the banality of the direct approach, also explore variants. "How long have you been Jewish?" asks one nosy young man. "Longer than you have" I reply. "Why did you become Jewish?" asks another voyeur. "Because it seemed the logical thing to do at the time" is my normal response.

If I was held up at gunpoint and asked the same question, I would have to say that I am not at all sure why I became Jewish. I had come from the U.K. to the U.S. as a post-graduate student at M.I.T. I was a long way from home; and I was in an extremely alien society, both inside and outside of the university. The U.S. and Europe have become culturally closer since, but then it was like going to Mars. Racial segregation still existed in the South. My old ordered life had gone and I found that, as the cliché has it, my horizons were expanding—but in a rather haphazard and undirected manner.

I was forced into my first attempt at independent living and budget-balancing. Life was an ever-changing challenge. Americans used to think much more broadly than Europeans. I had arrived in the U.S. as a fairly religious, church-attending Christian whose faith was based on an intellectual approach; but U.S. churches were as alien to me as much of the rest of the society. They seemed to be all veneer and no faith.

Then, I was at an age when marriage began to be something to consider. How would I ever find someone to marry out of my new range of acquaintances? How did anyone ever decide? It was a breathless, confusing time, a Vietnam War and flower-children time, and I was a fairly stolid British young man and a "Tech Tool" to boot.

What was one to think and do? Life went on, but my only real goal was to get my doctorate over and done with. I also had a constant, almost subconscious feeling that it was time to get myself sorted out a bit already. By my standards, I was practically a drifter.

One summer I had a job working in a company with an Orthodox Jewish engineer. He was a warm and brilliant man who was willing to talk. I could see that he had a genuinely ordered life and real goals, without being a dogmatic, priest-ridden peasant. Judaism clearly had something to it. Jews had never really come into my life before. My parents were not anti-Semitic, although they did call a Jaguar car a Jew's Rolls Royce. I had always lived in Jew-free areas. I had wondered occasionally how the Jews could possibly not have believed in our Messiah. What an opportunity missed—surely they must have regretted it by now, with all their silly rules. In Boston there were lots of Jews, but very few religious ones. They didn't believe in anything...and with considerable fervor.

Life moved slowly on. I learnt a little more about Judaism, and I became intrigued by the Orthodox Jewish culture and lifestyle. There was something very attractive in its certainties to an intellectually and culturally foot-loose young man. But there was no spiritual awakening; and the sheer effort required to become Jewish was something I wouldn't even have considered at the time.

Then came my motorcycle accident. I was near death and took a long time recuperating. My Jewish friends came to visit. I had time to think.

Eventually I was introduced to the Bostoner Rebbe and was impressed. Not only was this all a very sensible and organized approach to life, albeit a strange one; but also it had special people like him in it. If someone like the Bostoner Rebbe could believe in this somewhat bizarre faith, there had to be something to it.

Like a good Tech Tool, I thought operationally like an engineer. I didn't have visions. I didn't have spiritual experiences. I didn't "ooh" and "ah" about how wonderful and uplifting it all was. I just thought that this might be a rather good idea. The intellectual caliber of the young people around the Rebbe clearly demonstrated that other people, whose intelligence I could respect, also felt it was a good idea.

I had always believed in G-d, so that was no problem for me (although it often is for others). However, expressing that belief, or even realizing that it carries commitments, was not something that I had previously been aware of. Now I was.

So I did it. It seemed, as I said earlier, the logical thing to do at the time. It also felt good. Ah, my questioner leaves disappointed; but why does truth always have to be dramatic, bigger than life? What happened to the small still voice that works slowly but surely beneath the substratum of the prosaic? Isn't truth enough?

So I'll tell you instead about my first *seder* by the Bostoner Rebbe, *shlita*, an occasion I'll never forget, and one people won't let me forget. It's about as close as I can get to drama in *sotto voce*.

I had been married only a few weeks before, which was traumatic enough. Then came the *seder*, a complicated affair full of many details I had difficulty grasping let alone enjoying. I had to consume vast quantities of handmade *matzah*, which seemed more like burnt cardboard. This I had to wash down with umpteen glasses of sweet wine.

The Rebbe did his best to keep all his guests concentrated on the *seder*. The magnificent *niggunim* remain with me, my children and grandchildren to this day. The *droshos* were at a level that even I could follow, and my wife still remembers one of them. The enthusiasm of all present was inspiring. But the wine and the *matzah* gradually overcame me.

Some of the *matzah* didn't stay with me very long, but what was left wreaked havoc on my ordinarily stainless-steel digestive system. The four large cups of wine left me completely dazed. Finally the *seder* ended with a resounding rendition of *Chad Gadya* and I headed for my apartment.

Ah, there was the problem. The "I" and not the "we;" the "my" and not the "our." After the *seder* my wife had gone off to help the Rebbetzin. In my rather vague state, and in the absence of any visible reminder of my wife's existence, I had completely forgotten I was married. I simply left, newly wed and alone! One can't remember everything.

I should perhaps leave out the details of what happened when my wife finally did return to "our" apartment. Anyone with a sufficiently vivid imagination can fill in the details. To this date I do not think I have managed to have a *seder* without this unsavory little episode being retold for the benefit and further edification of any guests present. I fear this tradition may pass down the generations. "Do you remember Bubbie telling us how Zayde went home without her after the *seder* at the Bostoner Rebbe's?" Hopefully by then the true reason will have been forgotten, and everybody will assume that it was the overwhelming spiritual experience that led to my distraction.

I went to many other *sedarim* at the Rebbe's in the years that followed. I grew hardened to an extent to *shmura matzah* and wine. I remembered to go home with my wife. The complexities of the *seder* became routine, and the *seder* itself became a joy. As a *ger tzeddek* I have no family traditions and *minhagim*. Normally this is not something I worry about; it even has its advantages. However, at Pesach time, everyone else in the Jewish world returns to his or her parents or grandparents or *mechutonim*, and the *seder* is very much a festival of family continuity. This is the time when I genuinely regret lacking any continuity of my own. I do my best, of course. I tell my children that I don't eat "*gebrochts*" (*matzah* dipped in water) during Pesach because their *heilige zayde* (i.e., the Rebbe) never did. For some reason however, despite the truth of this statement, they never accept it as a valid answer.

The Bostoner Rebbe and his family have always been very conscious of this problem faced by so many of their "adopted children." With consummate skill, and without patronizing in any way, they always did their best to fill the gap, particularly at Pesach time. We were all part of the family and the Rebbetzin put us to work just like everyone else.

The Rebbe and Rebbetzin were not only surrogate parents, but also surrogate grandparents and more. It has been twenty-seven years since I was last at the Rebbe's *seder*, but I still feel the link between my *seder* of today and his *seder* then. I can almost believe myself to be continuing a family tradition, just like everyone else. Surely, when I was very small, I must have asked the *Mah Nishtana* in Dorchester, Massachusetts (hometown of the Rebbe)?

• • •

HER STORY.

My husband and I date from the "early years," not long after the Bostoner Rebbe and Rebbetzin moved to Brookline in 1962. I had tried Shabbos at the Rebbe's and became hooked in my junior year at Brandeis. Similarly, my husband-to-be was introduced to Beis Pinchas when he came to M.I.T. We met towards the end of 1966, and if anyone can be said to have been our *shadchan*, it was the Rebbe. But we've forgiven him long since.

Because I was a baalas teshuvah in the days before parents regarded that sort of aberrant behavior sympathetically, and because my husband was a *ger*, neither of us had family support. The Rebbe and Rebbetzin, therefore, became our surrogate parents, as they have been to countless others after us. They advised us on our wedding guest list, and they persuaded the caterer to give us a significant discount. The Rebbetzin took me to her own *sheitelmacher* and arranged for a discounted price there, too. Well, it's been over thirty years and I've forgotten a lot of what they did but, believe me, nothing was lacking. They even warned me to write into the musician's contract that he wasn't to sing, a wise precaution.

Given the circumstances, and the brief four days from our meeting until our engagement—just like our childrens' decades later—there was a certain romantic aura about our match. And, having had so much to do with it, the Rebbe was as delighted as the most devoted of parents.

Now and then he used to be visited by a freelance reporter from the *Morgen-Journal*, the only *frum* Yiddish paper of the time (now defunct), on the lookout for a bit of news. During one of these visits, after bringing the reporter up to date with all the activities at the New England Chassidic Center—for even then the Rebbe was involved in many different Jewish endeavors—the Rebbe happened to mention our upcoming *chasuna*. He didn't go into detail, but merely mentioned it as an aside.

The reporter, a true Yiddish writer, ignored entirely all the information about the shul and the Rebbe's efforts. He went off and wrote up the romantic tale of the *ger* and the baalas teshuvah. Can you blame him? The baal teshuvah phenomenon had hardly begun and, if we had wanted to, no doubt we could have made a living as after-dinner speakers, telling our tale; but we simply wanted to get on with life. We, of course, knew nothing of the visit. We knew the name of the *Morgen-Journal*, and, although I could have read it, I wouldn't have understood much. And then the fatal issue appeared, with a long, lavish article about us, based on few if any facts.

The Rebbe made a clean breast of the whole thing, and kindly translated the article for us. How we laughed! Most of it was pure fiction. I don't have the article, although I bet the Rebbe does. Among other flights of fancy I remember that it claimed I came from a home so rich that it was *eingetunken in foigelmilch* ("drowning in bird-milk"). I only wish. The rest of the story was in the same vein, picturing us as having thrown away a cushy, materialistic world to live in poverty and *frumkeit*.

The whole thing was hugely embarrassing particularly since people who knew us might think that we had fed the reporter all that nonsense. But the Rebbe said bracingly, "Don't worry at all. Nobody who reads the *Morgen-Journal* would know you."

That certainly made sense. Boston wasn't heavy on Yiddish-speakers and we had little contact with non-Bostonians. Unfortunately, our complacency turned out to be a fool's paradise. For the whole next year we kept running into people who had seen that article and who either knew us or who had put two and two together. It took a long time to live down all that hype!

It was hard to blame anybody, knowing how astonishing it was at that early date for two young people to choose an Orthodox lifestyle. I even wish that more of that article had been true. Especially the part about having been *eingetunken in foigelmilch*. True, we have been blessed with other kinds of riches, but would it have hurt?

THEN THAT'S PRETTY GOOD

Gerim (convert) stories usually limit themselves to describing all kinds of wonderful change. Young men and women "see the light" and move from an old, unhappy life of darkness to a new, happy life of light. Such simplified idealizations often ignore the fact that real *gerim* are real people, with real and often quite happy pasts, and decades spent growing up in a wonderful, loving, albeit non-Jewish family. While that does not negate the need to follow wherever truth leads, it does make change more painful than most people can imagine—particularly if you feel you are hurting people you sincerely love and who sincerely love you. At least, that was my experience.

Nobody wants to disappoint her parents, especially not me. I had been raised by generous, hardworking, community-minded parents. I knew what was proper and what was expected. At first my parents regarded my study of Judaism as just another fad; but once they realized that I was really serious and that conversion was a real option, my actions and attitudes hurt them constantly. That was certainly not my intent, but I was hurting them nonetheless. For example, I had to exclude myself from family gatherings that occurred on Shabbos and *Yom Tov*, and I wasn't available for our family's lifecycle events that took place in our church. Family and friends would ask my parents, "Where is she?" I knew it was hard on them; and that was hard on me.

My last conversation with my mother about the pain my Jewish religious lifestyle and spiritual decisions were causing her took place soon after my graduation from college. All my mother spoke about were her feelings of being betrayed and my abandoning my own family. I tried to explain that I was not unaware of or ungrateful for my good past. Indeed, my good upbringing was being reinforced by my Torah lifestyle. I led a "kosher" life, one she and my father could also be proud of. I was active in the community, the synagogue community. I had a job and was living up to my financial obligations. I insisted that the life I was living was one my parents could, and hopefully would, be proud of. Then the whole emotional thing hit me. What must *she* be feeling?

"Mom, this has nothing to do with my loving my family. You and Dad have been wonderful, supportive...really outstanding parents. I'm very lucky to be your child, proud to be your child. I'm not trying to hurt you and Dad. I'm only trying to get closer to G-d, and this is what I need to do to achieve this. My being Jewish is not about how much I love my family. It's about loving G-d."

My mother had been meeting with her old minister, who had been our family's pastor in my youth. She told me one of his comments: "You know, Judaism is not exactly a fly-by-night organization. It's been around for a long, long time." This gave her some comfort. She could understand that the behavior and traditions I had taken on were, in their own way, valid and part of a proven religious culture.

Eventually, my immediate family made every effort to accommodate my changing lifestyle and to include me. This was certainly far above and beyond the call of family duty. Functions were arranged so that I could attend, and my folks gave me more responsibility in arranging the food for family gatherings. It wasn't easy, but my folks were amazing. In fact, they still make sure that the whole biological family is represented at every *simchah*. My family is a real treasure. They were willing to invest time in our relationship; and, somehow, we worked it out.

Our friends from the shul community are our local family. We know we can count on them, and they know they can count on us. Many of these families make us a part of their *simchas* and are *machanech* my children. Most of these families have a close connection to the Bostoner Rebbe, *shlita*, and his family, who were so instrumental in my own education and conversion process.

I have always wanted my parents to be more comfortable with my choice to be Jewish. This acceptance has finally come, somewhat paradoxically, from my marrying a wonderful man who is devoted to Torah study and raising our family. My parents can see that I am putting energy into my family, my community and into good deeds such as charity, things I learned from their example. I have also been blessed with great kids who are active in the community and are growing up to be people my parents can be proud of. *Baruch Hashem* my life has not turned out to be an embarrassment for either *Klal Yisrael* or my parents. The risk that *Klal Yisrael* took on me seems to be paying off!

In fact, several years ago, the children and I visited my parents. I had planned to take a bus from their home to the Catskill Mountains to visit friends from Boston. Instead, my father volunteered to drive us there. A four-hour drive to the mountains with three preschool girls and a grown daughter, all of whom chose the path of *Yiddishkeit*, is not something any non-Jewish grandfather should miss. My Dad and I were trying to figure out some common ground. Where was I heading with my life, he wondered, with *his* grandchildren?

I was trying to explain what I wanted for my children—the pureness of their spirits, the wholesome life that was reinforced by a Torah lifestyle. He continued to drive and drive, but my point was not being made. Then he began looking at all the weird "American" teenagers hanging out at the malls on Route 42. Suddenly two Beis Yaakov-type girls, in modest denim skirts, long-sleeved jerseys and a fresh clean look came to the corner to wait for their camp bus.

These two *frum* young Jewish women were so noticeably different from other teens. Only their ears were pierced, and they radiated a calm, clean pleasure at the adventure of being on vacation. My dad slowed, looked at these two girls and then softly said, "Is that what you want my granddaughters to look like? Is that what you want them to become?"

"Yes, Dad. That's it."

"Well then, that's pretty good."

I think Hashem sent those girls. I think they may even have been angels. My Dad and I have never had words about my Judaism or the way my husband and I plan to raise our children since.

GLOSSARY

Alef-Beis	Hebrew alphabet; first two letters of the alphabet
Aliyah	Honor of being called up for the reading of a Torah portion (pl. *aliyos*)
Baal teshuvah	Lit. Master of Repentance, one who becomes religiously observant (f. baalas teshuvah)
Balabatish	Lit. "Master-of-the-House-like," something which is as expected for a respectable lay member of the community
Bar Mitzvah	Celebration of boy reaching 13, the age he is subject to *mitzvos*
Baruch Hashem	Blessed is G-d!
Bechirah	Choice
Beis din	Court operating in accordance with Jewish law
Beis medrash	Lit. house of learning, where Torah is studied (often combined with a shul)
Beis Yaakov	Religious Jewish girls' school system with high Orthodox standards
Bekeshe	Long, black frock coat, worn by Chassidic men
Bima	Reader's desk in the synagogue
Bnei Torah	Religiously observant men, esp. those with a solid yeshivah education
Bochur	Unmarried teenage boy of yeshivah age (pl. *bochurim*)
Brachah	Blessing

Bubbie	Grandmother (also: *Babeh*, *Bobeh*, etc.)
Chabad	System of Chassidus formualted by Shneur Zalman of Liadi (late 1700s) the first Lubavitcher Rebbe.
Chassid	Follower of a Chassidic Rebbe (pl. Chassidim)
Chassidus	Chassidism, Jewish religious movement started by R. Yisroel Baal Shem Tov (late 1700s)
Chasunah	Wedding
Chazzan	Leader of public prayer
Cheder	Religious school for young children (pl. *chedarim*)
Chessed	Deeds of kindness
Chizuk	Strengthening, encouragement
Cholent	Stew, usually served on Shabbos
Chumash	The Five (*Chamesh*) Books of the Torah
Chutzpadik	Acting with chutzpah (nerve, arrogance)
Daf Yomi	Widely accepted program for learning one folio page of Talmud each day
Daven	Pray
Drashah	Lecture or sermon elaborating a religious text or theme (pl. *drashos*)
Eretz Yisroel	Land of Israel
Febrengen	Lit. a gathering, particularly of Chabad (Lubavitcher) Chassidim

Frum	Religiously observant
Frumkeit	Religiosity
Gabbai	Shul functionary, esp. the one responsible for handing out *aliyos* etc.
Gemach	Charitable association
Gemara	Analyses and discussions of the Mishnah by later authorities (circa 200-500 CE)
Ger	Convert (pl. *gerim*)
Get	Bill of divorce
Goy	Non-Jew (pl. *goyim*)
Haftorah	Portion from the Prophets read on Shabbos
Hakafos	Circular procession and dancing with the Torah scrolls on Simchas Torah
Halachah	Jewish law
Halachic	In accordance with Jewish law
Haredi	Lit. trembler, one who is very devout and strict in his religious observance
Hashem	Lit. The Name, circumlocution for "G-d"
Hashkofah	A specific religious philosophy and lifestyle (pl. *hashkofos*)
Hatzlocha	Success
Heimish	Comfortable, warm approach typical of the religious community at large

Kaballah	Lit. accepted traditions, Jewish mysticism
Kaddish	Prayer praising Hashem, publicly recited during the first year (usually 11 months) of a close relative's passing
Kallah	Bride
Kapote	Long, black frock coat, worn by Chassidic men
Kashrus	Ritual supervision of foods (see kosher)
Kavod	Honor
Kedushah	Holiness (adj. *kodesh*)
Kever	Grave
Kiddush	Special benediction said over wine on Shabbos
Kiddush Hashem	Lit. Sanctification of the Name, behavior that raises public appreciation of Hashem
Kippa	Small head covering or skullcap for men
Kitzur	Lit. Summary, usually referring to the *Kitzur Shulchan Aruch*, an abridgement of the laws of the Jewish home
Klal Yisroel	The Jewish People
Kollel	Post-yeshiva learning institution for (esp. young) married men
Kosel	Western Wall of the Temple Mount in Jerusalem
Kosher	Ritually fit (esp. foods)
Kugel	Noodle casserole, often served on Shabbos

L'chaim	Lit. "To Life!," traditional Jewish toast
Machanech	Educator
Mamash	Really!
Matzah	Flat unleavened bread, eaten on Passover
Mazal	Luck
Mazel tov	Good luck! Congratulations!
Mechitza	Partition, esp. the one dividing the women and men's sections of a shul
Mechutan	In-law, relationship between the parents of the bride and the groom (pl. *mechutanim*)
Melacha	Lit. work, any one of the 39 categories of forbidden activity on Shabbos (pl. *malachos*)
Mikvah	Ritual bath (pl. *mikvaos*)
Milchig	Food containing milk or milk-derivatives, and thus forbidden to be eaten with meat
Minhag	Custom (pl. *minhagim*)
Minyan	Quorum of ten Jews needed for communal prayer (pl. *minyanim*)
Mishnah	Classic authoritative compilation of traditional Jewish laws, the foundation of the Talmud
Mitzvah	Righteous or religiously required deed (pl. *mitzvos*)
Mohel	Expert in performing religious circumcision (*bris milah*)
Musaf	Prayer service immediately following the Morning Service (*Shacharis*) on Shabbos and Yom Tov

Mussar	Moral teachings to improve one's character traits
Neshamah	Soul
Niggun	Melody (pl. *niggunim*)
Nusach	Order of prayer (the two main textual traditions are *Nusach Sefard* and *Nusach Ashkenaz*)
Parshah	Weekly reading from the Torah
Peyos	Curls of hair (side-locks) worn by Chassidic men to emphasize their adherence to the Biblical injunction not to shave round the corners of the head.
Pirkei Avos	*Chapters of the Fathers*, a collection of *Mishnayos* preserving the ethical advice of the Rabbinic leaders of that era, often specifically read on Shabbos afternoon.
Rav	Rabbi, esp. one expert in religious law
Rebbe	Chassidic rabbi and leader
Rebbetzin	Wife of a Rebbe
Seder	Lit. order, the ordered set of prayers and accompanying festive meal for Pesach eve
Shabbos	The Holy Sabbath (Friday night and Saturday)
Shadchan	Matchmaker
Shamash	Sexton of a shul
Shas	Abbreviation of *Shishah Sedarim* (The Six Orders), the Talmud
Sheital	Wig

Sheitalmacher	Wigmaker
Shidduch	Match (pl. *shidduchim*), the process of a making a match
Shlita	Abbreviation for *Sh'yichyeh L'Orech Yamim Tovim, Amen.* (May he live long and good days, Amen.) Customarily added after the name of a Rebbe.
Shmonah-Esrei	Lit. eighteen, the eighteen Rabbinically ordained benedictions forming the core of each prayer service
Shofar	Ram's horn blown on Rosh Hashanah
Shomer Shabbos	Keeping the laws forbidding work on Shabbos
Shteibel	Small, often informal shul
Shtreimel	Flat, fur-rimmed hat worn by Chassidic men on Shabbos and Yom Tov
Shul	Synagogue, Jewish house of worship
Shulchan Aruch	Code of Jewish Law, compiled by R. Yosef Karo (circa 1555 CE)
Siddur	Prayer book
Simchah	Joyous occasion
Siyum	Celebration marking the completion of the study of a religious text, esp. Talmud
Tallis	Fringed shawl (usually wool) worn by Jewish men during prayer
Talmid Chacham	Torah scholar
Talmud	Basic corpus of Jewish law (circa 200 BCE–500 CE), consisting of the Mishnah and Gemara

Tanach	The books of the Torah, *Neviim* (Prophets) and *Kesuvim* (Writings) taken as a whole
Tefillin	Small, black, leather boxes containing Torah passages written on parchment, worn by Jewish men during prayer
Tehillim	Psalms
Teshuvah	Repentance, spiritual return
Tikkun	Lit. repair, spiritual repair and restoration
Tish	Lit. table, Chassidic gathering at the Rebbe's meal
Toivel	To ritually immerse in a *mikveh*
Torah	Five Books of Moses; more broadly, the whole corpus of authentic Jewish tradition
Treif	Non-kosher
Tzaddik	Saintly person (fem. *tzedekes*; pl. *tzaddikim*)
Tzedakah	Charity
Tzitzis	Knotted woolen strings (fringes) attached to the four corners of the *tallis*
Yahrzeit	Anniversary of the passing of a loved one
Yerushalayim	Jerusalem
Yeshivah	School for advanced religious studies
Yeshivishe	Reflecting the attitudes of the Litvishe yeshivah world
Yichus	Lineage, esp. distinguished descent

Yid	Jew (pl. *Yiddin*), colloq.
Yiddishkeit	Judaism
Yirei Shamayim	Lit. Fearers-of-Heaven, devout Jews
z"tl	*Zecher tzaddik l'bracha*, May the memory of the righteous be blessed
Zayde	Grandfather
Zechus	Merit
Zocheh	To merit
Zohar	Basic classical Jewish mystical text, written by R. Shimon Bar Yochai